Unueco Partio: Creating a Single World Currency

Joshua W. Adams

ISBN-10: 1537145274
ISBN-13: 978-1537145273

DEDICATION

I dedicate this book to my friends and family who have supported me throughout my journey in discovering myself and my potential contributions to the world . I have been blessed to have their love. Also, this book are for all of those who work hard but feel their life is a struggle, that the current system is unable to meet their needs, and has been unable to also unlock their fullest potentials.

CONTENTS

INTRODUCTION

Unueco Partio is an organization and a movement I've hoped to start for some time. I believe the world is in need of a new way of civic engagement. Unueco Partio hopes to be a grassroots effort in many parts of the world whose purpose is to either start entirely new political movements which do not seem political, or to transform current institutions to meet the Unueco Partio standard. Unueco Partio stands for "Unity Party" and unity is the #1 value. No matter where you live, there are people everywhere in the world with similar goals, dreams, and aspirations. No matter your belief system or non-belief system, you may share similar feelings, thoughts, and emotions. No matter your skin color or cultural identity, you may be the son, daughter, father, or parent of someone. We live in a shared humanity and our vision of governmental and social engagement should reflect this reality.

Unfortunately I am not very good at social organization. I am very strong at writing and teaching so I thought I would write a book which can establish some of the principles I hope to strive for Unueco Partio while focusing in on a specific purpose.

This book has a single goal, a single mission, and a single purpose: To rejuvenate the world body by creating a new economic model and supporting political system centered on the use of energy as the sole currency used throughout the world.

As I write this in 2016, there are many systematic maladies in the world body, many diseases which our current systems have created and thus are ill-equipped to provide the remedies. Some of the symptoms include the increasing number of governments over-burdening their citizens in ever-increasing debts, the impending ecological disasters which will eventually destroy all the progress civilization has made, and the instituting of inequality amongst the world's people have created a tenuous situation. I hope instead of change being forced upon us, in terms we would not agree

1

to but have no choice in accepting, we can willingly change course in such a way that is agreeable and conducive to the further development of this society.

To get there, I hope to weave a tapestry discussing faith, science, economics, finance, governance, and most importantly, the family. Some of this may seem academic, some of it personal, and I'm confident there will be something in here which will spur your imagination. I hope to keep each subject short and to the point without compromising the argument I hope to make. I admit I understand the sole purpose of an utterance is to influence, but even if I am unsuccessful in my aim, I do hope this can spur discussion, consultation, and a desire to help mankind in her aims. This is the Unueco Partio way. I hope this will be our way.

For any discussion with myself or others involving any subject discussed, or even the totality of this book, please join the blog and discussion forums under the Unueco Partio name. They can be found using a simple search through any search engine, WordPress, or Facebook.

Chapter 1
FINANCE: WHAT IS MONEY?

I wanted to start the first chapter going over the definition and usage of money. This won't be a textbook level, academic approach but instead my attempt at defining something as simple as I know how. Brevity without losing important details will be a goal of this entire book in each subject I describe.

Currently, money is used as a mode of transaction, an asset, and a receipt of debt. There are two main kinds of money in usage today. The first is commodity money, which we mostly know through silver and gold coins or other physical, durable metals. The second is fiat money, which we know as paper money whose value is determined by the government who issues the money. Often times through history both have been interlinked, such as the USA's greenback paper money being backed by gold reserves.

Commodity money is what had been used throughout most of history. A commodity is basically anything physical and durable which people of a society value. This has taken the form of grains, clam shells (like wampum), ivory tusks, precious metals, gems, salt, and even furs. The reason why durable goods were used for trade was because often times, true bartering was impossible. True bartering required two people (or parties) who each had something the other needed or wanted. Since this was improbable, these durable commodities developed as forms of "IOU's" that could be redeemable later or elsewhere.

Commodity money often ran into long-term issues. One situation would be scarcity of the commodity. If someone or a group of people had access to most of the commodity, there would be an initial unequal distribution of wealth. Often times governments, no matter how primitive or sophisticated, would secure those commodities. The price of the commodity itself would go up, causing the value of other goods to depreciate. This would could cause poverty and eventual revolutions.

Another situation would be if the commodity was easily reproducible. If nature recreated the commodity quite quickly, such as with clam shells, then the society would have high inflation. The more money introduced, the lower the value of the money would become but the more expensive other goods would be. This also was unsustainable. One interesting scenario is when the Spanish secured the silver mines from the Inca in the 16th century. At first Spain become relatively wealthy as compared to other European nations and China, nations who valued silver as a commodity. Then due to hyperinflation, the economy and Spanish society quickly faltered and grew relatively weak.

Some commodity money became relatively sophisticated, such as when the Greeks first made currency. Currency is basically anything created which has an agreed upon value backed by a government. Currency was usually a precious metal at a specified weight and stamped with an inscription. One purpose of a government creating currency was to make it easy to set taxes, which the taxes in turn created a need for merchants to use the said currency. Still, these currencies being based on commodities would eventually suffer the same fates as prior commodity money. Sometimes other complications arose, such as when a new leader would be established who wanted his or her own image stamped on the currency. Old currency would immediately be worthless, sometimes even made illegal to use. This happened very often in China, and sometimes merchants would totally ignore the new currency and use original, unstamped precious metals to trade. This instability in government monetary policy would lead to large gyrations in the economic and financial activities of the citizenry, which also led to difficulty in the government receiving adequate tax income to finance public projects.

Sometimes a government's policies, such as with international affairs, would lead to changes in how money was used. What happens when a government goes to war and the costs of war are more than the government can collect and pay upon? Soldiers won't fight for free and soldiers needed regular supplies to be combat effective. Governments would need to introduce fiat money in place of the scarce commodity. Fiat money originally took the form of IOUs on paper, like in 11th century China, which soldiers could later redeem if their side won the war. If they lost, well, they were put into a bad situation. These IOUs were both a debt as well as a money. See, originally debt was money and money was debt. Neither were intended to be stores of wealth or assets, although in modern accounting practice, a liability must have always had an equaling asset. Of course "equity" changed the equation some but most people understands the basics.

Unfortunately in the earliest cases, fiat money was based on the premise the government could guarantee the value of the paper. This would almost inevitably lead to governments being emboldened to issue more debt than they could legitimately afford and once again lead to either the government's demise or very bad economic conditions for those who had devalued money due to inflation. In modern times, most of the world uses fiat money whose value is not tied to any commodity. There are, as of this writing, 180 currencies in use across the world. All of them are fiat money. This means there are 180 different valuations governments give their money, 180 different governments who can create money as needed to fund debt, and 180 different ways people have to determine the value of a currency as compared to another. Sounds complicated, right? It is.

For several years I experimented with foreign currency exchange. I actually had some success and for 6 months, traded my friends' money and earned them about 17% income each month. It was time consuming so I stopped. However, what I did learn from the years of studying foreign currency exchange is this:

1.   Experts really have no clue what is going on. If I followed expert advice I always would lose money. Also, a certain news would move valuations in different directions by different amounts, sometimes temporarily. Volatility, to me, means experts and the markets that rely on experts have no real intellectual basis. This is merely passion and imagination.

2.   Foreign currency exchange is a zero sum game. This means for any $1 earned, another $1 would be lost somewhere within the market. The total sum of all gains and losses was zero. This again shows the market is once again based on passion and imagination.

3.   You could seriously make money if you could anticipate how the market's passions and imaginations could play out. This was more a study in behaviorism and psychology than economics and finance, although one could argue economics and finance is really a behavioral science. Still, I find making money in foreign currency exchange intriguing despite the feeling I should never be able to make money based on passion and imagination. It was like making money by saying Santa Claus exists. Oh wait, that market is also covered.

Notice I have very little respect for money markets and say they are merely passion and imagination. I invite anyone to prove to me otherwise. I would love to be convinced.

Today, we have a system where money is created by central banks run either by the government or by private institutions acting on behalf of the government. Within this framework, banks can become too big to fail such as during the 2007-2008 financial crisis in the USA, whereas governments can be too big to fail. This means the rules of creating debt and manipulating debt and money work differently for banks than for governments. Governments entertain increasing amounts of debt to keep the economy stimulated as per Keynesian economic theory (or its relatives) and governments entertain issuing money to achieve certain objectives, such as manipulating employment rates, interest, and inflation (as per monetary theory). None of this is sustainable.

For example, in many countries, a practice called fractional reserve banking exists. It started when goldsmiths would store people's gold in vaults and later realized people would never collect their gold at the same time. The goldsmiths would issue notes to state the value of the person's deposit, and would eventually use that gold to loan to others or invest in other business ventures. As long as there was enough gold to cover any redemptions, they were good. The goldsmiths would earn interest on what they loaned and was a good system temporarily. Eventually, since this was commodity money, the valuations would become volatile and sometimes people would want their gold all at the same time so as to secure its value. This is called a bank run. The goldsmith, and later banks, would go out of business. In the long-term, everyone realized this was an unsustainable business practice. In order to change up the business model to make it sustainable, governments were encouraged to establish central banks, such as the USA Federal Reserve. The Fed would establish regulations as to how much currency the bank would have to keep on hand, insure deposits, and also provide lending to the banks. This was the clever part. Anytime a bank would lend out more money than it had available, the Fed would loan more money to the bank. This money would be at a very low interest rate, at least lower than a citizen could get on the market, and the Fed would create new money to cover that loan.

Eventually all economic activity in the USA has relied on the stability of this system. To create new money, there must be new loans made by private banks, also known as new debt. To ensure inflation wouldn't get too high, the Fed established a guidance that 2% annual inflation is optimal to spur economic growth. The Fed would change interest rates to encourage or discourage the creation of new debts to meet the 2% inflation goal. This system often seems fairly stable but as we saw in the 2007-2008 financial crisis, this has led to some very bad accounting procedures due to the passions and imagination of the financiers and normal citizens.

Consequence 1: The value of money must go up 2% forever. This value potential is infinity or until time ends, whichever happens first. Is this sustainable? No, unless your imagination can also go on forever.

Consequence 2: The creation of money is an interlinked dynamic between banks, the government, and each manipulating the demand for money. Due to volatility, we understand the demand for money, whose valuation is based on passion and imagination, the demand must also be based on passion and imagination.

Consequence 3: An entire economic system has been created to cater to exciting these passions and imaginations, which we have seen is extremely unstable. Read any business and finance section of a news source and each day you'll see reasons for why markets go up and down. A rational person would understand a variable of one day does not erase the variable of a prior day, or expected variables in the future. The lack of logic and reason is astounding. Also, you understand the underlying reality of fear. Often times we fear what we do not understand or know, and this is especially true when in relation to trying to anticipate other people's passions and imaginations. Extremely hard to understand.

Consequence 4: No one knows the entire amount of debts they have. Everyone knows how much money they have, but debts they do not. When the deleveraging of debt occurred, no one still ever figured out the totality of debts. Even today no government understands the amounts of debts which exist although money supply is created. This means the original intention of debt being money and money being debt no longer exists. This discrepancy will eventually cause the entire system to collapse.

Consequence 5: Most governments today, to include the most local governments of school districts, townships, counties, provinces, villages, cities, and so forth have unsustainable debts. These governments will all eventually collapse unless the system changes. In the state of Illinois for example, financial institutions rated the state's bonds as near junk. This causes the state to pay higher interest up until the point of expected bankruptcy. A government can be bankrupt to a bank, but a bank cannot be bankrupt to a government. Governments have failed, but so far governments have not allowed large banks to fail. Could this lead to financial institutions governing? For now they control all the resources of passion and imagination, since 99% of all people in the world have bought into this system. One could argue this is already the case.

Consequence 6: Actions in society which are vital to the sustainability and progress of all mankind are steeped in neglect and poverty. One example is the plight of the world's farmers. Mankind needs food, food is real, food makes us healthy and feel good, yet we value food less than other goods within our demand of passions and imagination. This will cause an ecological disaster where mankind will fight amongst themselves for vital resources because these resources were neglected as being important today.

Consequence 7: Inequality, especially economic inequality, continues to increase. This has already sparked revolutions in areas where the passions and imaginations of wealth and fiat money led to the neglect of millions who were faced with surviving in the face of drought, such as in Syria and Libya. This inequality has reduced mankind's compassion and ability to act when there is compassion. We look down upon those who do not succeed in our system of passion and imagination and treat them as crazy, lazy, and inferior. Worst of all we treat them as criminals and outcasts.

One could argue under this system, we have made a lot of progress. Innovation is high because innovators get to share in the success, people do live longer, there is currently more peace than there ever has been, and some nations are able to successfully provide for the poor's needs. I totally agree with these progressions made and I definitely do not want to lose all that we have gained. I also argue that we can do better. We can do better than capitalism, we can do better than communism, and we can do better than any system we have allowed our passions and imagination to create.

Chapter 2
FAITH: GOLDEN RULES RELATED TO MONEY

In this section, I want to go over some seemingly universal teachings in the world's religions which relate to money, economy, and the practices thereof. Many people are familiar with the well-known Golden Rule in which many cultures in recorded history taught. This rule is placing the neighbor, or immediate other, in the same place as yourself. Here is an example from Tao scripture: "Regard your neighbor's gain as your own gain, and your neighbor's loss as your own loss."— T'ai Shang Kan Ying P'ien

I selected this one as it uses words we commonly associate with our economic and financial activities. Also, we could easily substitute similar words, such as the word profit for gain. One can imagine who the neighbor is. For an individual this could be a person next-door, or if we are thinking within the realm of organized society, we may imagine a neighboring town, neighboring state or province, and even a neighboring country.
"Regard Mexico's profit as the United States' profit, and Mexico's loss as the United States' loss."

I understand such a transmutation of the Golden Rule from individual to a nation seems strange and is in a minority viewpoint, but even nations are merely made of many individuals. A majority of the world's people claim adherence to a belief system which teaches the Golden Rule, yet all of our political and economic systems are based on the exact opposite notion. This conflict between belief and action, in my estimation, is the biggest source of conflict amongst the world body. However, let me digress for now away from what could seem like preaching.

It is interesting to discover there are other mini-Golden Rules which exist in the world's faiths which relate to money and economics. Let me state a few that I want to cover in this section.

1. Acceptance on using money
2. Acceptance on working
3. Encouragement to give charity
4. Prohibitions on Usury
5. Moderation
6. Detachment from material/physical things
7. Debt is a promise

Let me start with "Acceptance on using money." As far as I can see in the world faiths, there was never a prohibition on using money. Both Buddha and Jesus taught their disciples they did not need money in the path of enlightenment and service, but there was no greater prohibition on using money, no matter its form. The oldest documented written acceptance on the use of money was back in the time of Abraham, when he purchased 400 shekels of land with silver. Even with the most recently created world-wide faith, the Baha'i Faith, money is allowed.

There is also a universal acceptance to working. In many faiths, monasticism is an accepted and sometimes preferred pathway. I would point out that even in these lifestyles, there was often work being done although the work did not come with the ambition of seeking personal profit. Still, even in faiths where the monastic lifestyle is considered a pious path, such as in Buddhism and Catholicism, only a small minority of people follow this lifestyle. This is because the original teachings did not require monasticism. Followers were never prohibited to work for personal profit and the degrees of righteousness were later defined by later leaders of these faiths.

While it was universally accepted in the world's faiths that work is acceptable, there was always much more frequent guidance in the act of charity. In the Qur'an for example, there are more verses which discuss the merits of charity than in the guidance of prayer. In a way, charity is a form of worship. In some faiths there is a minimum amount of charity such as the 10% tithe, and in other instances the amount is at the discretion of the believer.

Charity at its very core is an embodiment of the Golden Rule. The idea behind charity is this, if a person has earned a profit through work or another means such as inheritance, the person can give a portion of this profit to another who needs it. The gift is without expectation of repayment and in every faith, the charity is preferred to be done in private so as to not draw attention to oneself. Charity should not exist because a person feels compelled to give for the sake of law or God's favor, but instead because the person truly desires a better outcome for the recipient. Charity, in 1 Corinthians of the New Testament, is often translated as love. Depending on language, charity is love and love is the embodiment and spirit behind the Golden Rule. Some faiths have included further guidelines about the nature of charity, such as to not give what you would not want to receive.

In every faith, there have been prohibitions on usury. Usury today is defined as an unnecessarily high interest rate on any loan. However, no faith has exactly determined what that exact rate would need to be to constitute as usury. There are banks in some Muslim countries which have eliminated interest completely. In this case, using no interest is a form of charity. Other faiths allow interest, but always prohibit usury. The issues with usury come from the loaner seeking so much profit from the debt that the borrower becomes a slave to that debt. In many historic societies, such as the Romans, a high debt which could not be paid led to direct ownership of the person. In Rome the slave could eventually be freed, but even in other societies it was virtually impossible to pay those debts because of the interest imposed. Today, some businesses such as loan sharks or even payday loaners make a practice of charging high interest and fees solely with their own interests in mind. This can lead to a cycle of poverty in populations which are already impoverished or susceptible to poverty.

Another universally common teaching in the world's faiths that can be applied to money is the practice of moderation. Moderation means to never take anything to an extreme, even if it is a good thing. The art of moderation forces people to pull back from the excess of passion or even the harms of deprivation. In the practice of charity, earning profits, working, earning interest, and other financial activities, moderation is a practice which can definitely be applied.

"Whoso cleaveth to justice, can, under no circumstances, transgress the limits of moderation. He discerneth the truth in all things, through the guidance of Him Who is the All-Seeing. The civilization, so often vaunted by the learned exponents of arts and sciences, will, if allowed to overleap the bounds of moderation, bring great evil upon men. Thus warneth you He Who is the All-Knowing. If carried to excess, civilization will prove as prolific a source of evil as it had been of goodness when kept within the restraints of moderation. Meditate on this, O people, and be not of them that wander distraught in the wilderness of error." (Baha'u'llah, Gleanings from the Writings of Baha'u'llah, p. 342)

Moderation, in this sample from the Baha'i Faith, suggests justice requires moderation and excesses will lead to the downfall of a society. Even though the context did not specify economics nor finance, today's society does include the study of these subjects as sciences. It is through their classification which I find relevancy.

The sixth mini-Golden Rule would be the practice of detachment. Detachment has many definitions but sometimes I like to define detachment as being emotionally removed from the outcomes of an action or from the object itself. It can also mean regardless of circumstances, your movements and character remain constant. In the context of detachment from physical and material goods, this emotionally removed state can mean a person does not evaluate one's self-worth based on these physical items. It could mean a person will not treat another differently no matter the quantity or quality of physical items that person has. In our applications of justice, especially in regards to money, it should be equal regardless the material circumstances of the person. Detachment helps make the example sentence I made using Mexico and the United States more realistic. Detachment removed material inequality from the equation. In usury, detachment would remove the outer appearance.

The final rule is that debt is a promise, an obligation. All faiths teach people to honor their commitments, to keep their promises, and in many circumstances, to pay their debts. Religion has never prohibited trade and has never prohibited debt, only usury. Trustworthiness is the foundation upon which all other values rest upon and debt can only exist if trustworthiness exists.

As you can see, these seven additional mini-Golden Rules operate within the realm of the well-known Golden Rule. They help refine the potentialities beyond that of the common practice of verbal kindness and polite manners. These rules help refine our actions, our energies, the way we orient ourselves within the greater context of "us." In the world of money, economy, and the systems of government we devised to regulate ourselves, we must not avoid these principles. You as the reader may have declared belief in one of the faith traditions which teach these rules and have begun to evaluate the seven consequences presented in Chapter 1. You may think about how your actions are within the seven rules and the seven consequences. You as the reader may not subscribe to any belief, or even deny the existence of God. In this case there is a chance you see how faith-based societies have fallen short of the ideals they teach and believe there are other approaches to establishing ethics. No matter the background, one cannot deny the current form of our economies, the usage of money, nor the political systems we've created. No matter the background, one cannot deny the commonality of teachings within Judaism, Zoroastrianism, Hinduism, Christianity, Buddhism, Islam, Taoism, the Baha'i Faith, and even local faiths amongst native peoples.

When I propose a single world currency, it is with these things in mind. Our systems are far from perfect and can be improved upon by applying principles 99% of us claim to believe in. We can collectively change the seven consequences, and others not even specified, into a world-wide Golden Age where we live the Golden Rules. This isn't capitalism. This isn't communism. This isn't any system devised. This will be Unueco Partio and you can help guide it.

Chapter 3
SINGLE WORLD CURRENCY: AN INTRODUCTION

Before I get into the ideas of using energy for a currency, I want to discuss the reasoning and purpose behind establishing a single world currency. Let me share a story from some travels I had been on.

Nearly a year ago, I travelled to Bangladesh. While in the city of Sylhet, I had Chicken Biryani at a fairly normal restaurant. It was not part of a hotel complex, everyone wore casual clothes, and there was a robust energy. Authentic. The price for the Biryani was about 320 Taka, which currently equates to about $4 USD. The same dish at a similar style restaurant in the USA will cost around $10, often times more. $10 dollars is 2.5 times more, or 250% more, than what I was able to get in Sylhet. Why can I afford more of the same thing in another country? Why can someone in Bangladesh afford less of the same thing in the USA? Is this a morally acceptable outcome?

This dynamic between international prices has been a topic of much interest by economists. One popular scenario to plot out is the price of the Big Mac worldwide, as this is an item made the same way in many countries of the world. This is called the Big Mac Index and was introduced by The Economist magazine in 1996. You can use this tool to see how currencies are valued. Further, you can use this to imagine the impacts of trade, wages, purchasing power, and monetary policy. As stated in Chapter 1, having over 180 different currencies being managed by 180 different countries, each with their own decision making processes, we can see this dynamic between currencies often change. Is this the free markets establishing the various valuations, or more like central authorities trying to move markets in desirable directions?

You see, we are told in many places throughout the world that the prices of everything is based upon supply and demand, factors of production such as the price of labor, labor's productivity, effective use of technology, and even geographical advantages. We are sometimes told in the business news and even in basic economics classes that the prices of things have little to do with the valuations of currencies, other than maybe the effects of inflation and the cost of borrowing. However, I do not believe the markets, even the freest markets, are actually free markets nor are they based much on supply and demand. I am going to break apart the components which make up the purchase of Chicken Biryani and see why the prices is 250% higher in the USA than in Bangladesh.

To order Chicken Biryani at a restaurant and to pay for it, there are similar components each restaurant must include within its business model. Each restaurant has to secure the ingredients from suppliers, there must be labor to prepare and serve the dish, and there must be overhead for the building and equipment itself, plus the cost of the land the building is on. Each must navigate various government regulations to ensure licensing, health standards, taxation, and accounting practices.

The land underneath both restaurants were different. The restaurant in the USA used more space, mostly for a sizeable parking lot. The Bangladesh restaurant had a smaller footprint, but also had 2 stories versus the one in the USA. It is definitely true land is much more expensive in the USA, and this restaurant was in a suburb. But, the demand for land in Bangladesh should be at a higher ratio than the supply. Why is land per acre more expensive for the USA restaurant even though there are fewer people per square mile/km in the USA? If the mechanism for supply and demand were the sole factors at play, one would think there would be higher prices for land in Bangladesh, and perhaps in general, more wealth being created through real estate valuations than in the USA. Could it be because Americans use much of their land for parking lots, such as with this restaurant? This could be true. Trying to find a place to park anything in Bangladesh is like trying to find my glasses in the dark after a great commotion. What makes a piece of land worth more than another? Bangladesh can grow three rice crops on undeveloped land in a year versus one crop in the USA. The natural undeveloped productivity of the lands the restaurants were built on would favor more value for the land in Bangladesh. Both restaurants had access to treated city water, modern sewage, electricity, and other modern amenities. I really cannot think of any reason valuations of land are higher in the USA unless there are other factors, such as the passion and imagination of the people in one country are different than that of the other. Maybe the cost of modern amenities is more in the USA for some reason.

What about the buildings themselves? In Bangladesh, the restaurant appeared to be made of steel reinforced concrete and was two stories tall. In the USA, the restaurant was a mix of steel and wood. Usually it costs more to build a multi-story building than a single story building due to the better foundation needed to support the structure, as well as other beams and pillars throughout the space. The concrete is a cheaper material than any steel used in the USA, but the wood is a highly renewable resource. I believe the wood should offset the cost of the steel. I think the cost to build from a materials standpoint would be somewhat equal given the circumstances and the availability of wood in the USA versus the availability of concrete, and the energy required to transport its higher weight. The durability of the buildings should be similar, although concrete suffers from erosion when exposed to a lot of rain, and can crack due to its inflexibility. Wood is organic and naturally decomposes unless it is treated with chemicals, adding to the cost. I will conclude the costs should be fairly equal.

What about the labor used to build the buildings? Using Bangladesh's manufacturing and foreign investment marketing, I see the average cost of labor in Bangladesh is about $.23 USD. The minimum wage in the USA is $7.25. This is about 30 times more expensive, and in the USA labor in construction is usually more like $15-$20 per hour. The overhead cost of labor is exceptionally greater in the USA versus Bangladesh. We know already a portion of this difference is the valuation in currency, but why is the gap in labor cost so high? We can look at the supply and demand of labor to start. Construction jobs are labor intensive, require demanding physical requirements, and some training in the various components of carpentry, welding, molding, plumbing, electric wiring, and so forth. Countrywide, Bangladesh has a population that is close to 50% that of the USA, although the population density of Bangladesh is 37 times that of the USA. This means for any local job in Bangladesh, there is a vast supply of people keeping wages low. I would also assume there is a great deal of competition in wage seeking, which can keep certain productivity measures low due to turnover and lack of investment in training. Although I must ask, if a person supposedly does equal work in Bangladesh and the USA, wouldn't the cost be the same? I know this is not how anything works, but I wanted to ask this question to grease the wheels.

What about the labor used to prepare and serve the food? I assume this would also fall into the same category as the labor used to build the restaurants, although it should be noted in the USA, the wage for waiters and waitresses drops substantially to $2.13, only 9 times the wage in Bangladesh. The servers in Bangladesh also do not expect a tip, although I personally gave them a tip as a means to show American culture.

What about the price of the rice? When I was in Bangladesh, the price of rice was about $.18 USD for one pound. The average price in the United States was about $.52 USD, less than 3 times the price in Bangladesh. Bangladesh does have a geographical advantage in producing rice as they are able to have up to 3 growing seasons per year. The potential 3 times of production per equal area could be the entire difference. Although culturally, it is interesting to note the demand for rice in Bangladesh is higher than nearly any other food. This could be due to the low price, but isn't supply and demand the major market factors? Once again, potentially not. In the USA, the price of labor is higher but the amount of labor used is small. As with much of American grain agriculture, rice production and harvesting has been mechanized. Mechanization requires the use of fuel, oil, and manufactured components. All of these have a high capital cost but theoretically increase overall return on investment through productivity gains. Also, both countries export rice on the world market, where prices should become relatively normalized due to competition. If domestic USA production of rice warrants retail pricing 3 times that of Bangladesh despite world market prices being the same, then either there is a price premium associated with selling in the USA, or Bangladesh is much more efficient at growing rice and is making more of a profit per pound than the USA does on the world market. I prefer to believe the higher cost of rice then, in the USA, is mostly due to the premium of prices. With wages being 30 times higher than in Bangladesh, Americans have more money to spend and thus sellers can adjust the prices upward to seek more profit. I will mention rice per pound has the same calories (energy content) and nutrition in each country, with slight amounts of variability due to quality of harvest and selective breeding.

I could go on with other food ingredients, such as the chickens, saffron, and so on, but I think you have a general idea the situation. Unprocessed food in Bangladesh is 3 times less than in the United States and prepared food is 30 times less expensive in Bangladesh. The majority of these price differences come through the cost of labor and the value of a currency. Both of these factors are based on one presumption and I am about to make a strong statement.

The people in the United States believe they are worth more than the people in Bangladesh. This is not a statement about prejudice, racism, nationality, or any other merit. This is why labor in the USA earn more and their money goes farther in Bangladesh. There are various institutions which help implement this belief, such as labor unions, regulations to ensure a minimum level of quality and safety, and most importantly, a high level of control on the flow and movement of working age people.

If a free market requires the flow of goods and services to be efficient, then the same should be true of labor. However, since 1924, the flow of labor into the United States had its first control with a quota being established to limit the flow of Russians, Southern Europeans, and Jews. Originally this was done to ensure the Western European majority remained so in the United States, but this eventually set in place a precedent which exists today. Today, there are quotas on the numbers and types of immigrants in every country. Skilled and professional labor is encouraged and unskilled labor is discouraged, although not eliminated. This, along with the low birth rate among Americans, has created a situation where wage levels are high due to the smaller supply of labor, and the creation of trade policies where jobs which require a low wage and unskilled labor have gone to countries like Bangladesh. Is this fair?

I say this is unfair for both Americans and Bengali people. For the Americans, they must invest heavily in higher education, technical trades, and other informal skills training to make a living in an environment of high costs associated with the idea Americans are worth more than other people in the world. For the Bengali, they have little hope of their institutions investing heavily in their education, technical trades, and other informal skills to increase their quality of work and move up the industrial ladder. Due to slightly higher birth rates and higher mortality rates of older people, there is a constant supply of workers being created within Bangladesh. Bengali people, due to how the economic system is, are worth less. As such, there is no sustainable hope to improve their levels of poverty without a massive reform. In both countries, due to the disconnect between the value of the individual and how capitalists value them, there are increasing levels of discontent in both societies.

If Americans have higher wages for the same work, why can't someone in Bangladesh compete for that job? If there are more low skill jobs in Bangladesh for Americans to work, why don't Americans go to Bangladesh? This would be a potential free market outcome if supply and demand were the only factors. Americans say we want jobs. Same as those in Bangladesh. The reason is because the institutions we have created do not allow those choices to be made unless governments approve those decisions according to the wills of their populace. There are many reasons why America has limited immigrants from one country more than the other, but it is the same process that makes Americans believe they are worth more than others. The economic system then, with its 180 nations governing 180 currencies, is dominated by a social construct that some people are worth more than others. I'll visit this idea later.

There are two ways to potentially bring about more equality into this world economically. One would be for the countries of the world to open their borders. This would be devastating to the current system in the short run. This could potentially shock ethnically isolated people with diverse cultures, much like when Mexico City became the world's first global city in the 1500's. This could potentially shock governments trying to deal with the immigrants trying to go to countries where the populations built institutions on the grounds of higher individual worth. Other countries could lose many citizens and taxpayers because their citizens want to leave dreadful conditions. In the long-run, governments would be forced to adapt and adjust, merging the world closer to equal rules.

The second solution would be to eliminate the diversions multiple currencies have created. Having one single currency would mean inflation in Bangladesh, currently around 10% each year, would not be higher than in the United States, which is about 2%. Bengali people each year are able to buy less, except for the upper middle class and wealthy, while the American can go to Bangladesh and live like royalty, even if the American is middle class in America. Inflation, if it is necessary, would be smoothed over throughout the entire world. Someone growing rice in Bangladesh could potentially earn the same as another growing rice in the United States. Instead of monetary policy and institutionalized valuations of self-worth determining prices, we'd have true competition. The profit one can earn is based on how effective they are at reducing costs and increasing productivity, or how effective they are at investing other resources. For those who argue a free market is the best method for economy, a single currency is the surest way to ensure every person in the globalized economy is playing by the same monetary rules.

Let me review a single currency against the 7 consequences.

Consequence 1: The value of money will still go up forever. Nothing changes.

Consequence 2: Right now banks and government would still manipulate the demand for money. Volatility could be less due to the certainty created by eliminating 179 other currencies.

Consequence 3: Exciting passions and imaginations would still exist, although fewer variables would exist to excite these passions. The true costs of things would be easier to analyze and compare across businesses throughout the world.

Consequence 4: It would become easier to understand the accounting associated with debts and money supply. It would take great work to understand a world-wide dynamic, but eliminating 179 currencies makes the job much easier.

Consequence 5: This probably would not change the issues governments are facing on its own. Having one single currency would not change many of the decisions governments and its people make, although better understanding of debt might create better market controls and better tools to guide fiscal policy.

Consequence 6: There would be much more equality in the value of labor, goods, resources, and so on. There would still be varying institutional and local factors which could affect local pricing, but I believe situations such as one person in the world earning 30 times the money for doing the same task as the other would be reduced. Equality of person would be more easily understood while allowing the dynamics for competition to exist.

Consequence 7: Inequality based upon nationality would reduce although the gap between the wealthy and the poor could still continue to increase. There would need to be other changes done to limit or reduce this gap.

What about the development of a single currency in regards to the 7 Golden Rules?

Golden Rule 1: Money would still be acceptable and the primary mode of transaction.

Golden Rule 2: Work would still be encouraged as a means to survive and profit one's self.

Golden Rule 3: Charity may not be encouraged by using a single currency, although the potential need for charity could be reduced by establishing equal rules and evaluating worth more consistently. Often times charity is needed due to how we value others, and charity is there to give more than we value. This is kind of a cruel way to think of charity, but it is true. Perhaps the key to reducing the need for charity is valuing others how they deserve to be valued, like a brother or sister.

Golden Rule 4: Usury would not be eliminated although there could be more worldwide competition for loans and debt now that the uncertainty of the valuation of money would be reduced. This increased competition could naturally reduce interest rates if the monetary policy allowed it. However, one should be warned that the role of banks in establishing monetary policy would not be reduced or eliminated solely by introducing a single world currency.

Golden Rule 5: Moderation would be the first effect of a single currency, although its effect could be temporary. The desire for physical goods or the ever increasing value of self would resume unabated. In the long run, moderation may not be any part of a single currency system as the spirit of people was not necessarily changed.

Golden Rule 6: There would be no natural increase in the practice of detachment due to the same reason moderation would not be changed. This is more of a spiritual condition. There could be detachment to the outcome of self-worth based upon national identity, ethnicity, or outer appearance due to a single currency system, but the spiritual aspect of detachment to physical goods and outcomes would most likely be the same.

Golden Rule 7: There would be no change in ensuring debt is a promise or a commitment one makes. By using better accounting practices in global activity could help ensure one does not make more promises than one can bear, the actual practice or people's stances towards debt probably would not change.

As you can see, introducing a single world currency can have some positive effects on the world economy and the plight of people world-wide. These effects would not be spiritual in nature, but would help allow free markets run more efficiently by making the process of establishing prices, identifying debt, managing the money supply, and simplifying competition for interest rates and money. We would not have to navigate myriads of differing and competing monetary policies throughout the world and instead value people, resources, goods, and services closer to their true worth. The concept of equilibrium often described in economics and finance would be closer to being a reality, if it ever could be real. Finally, passions and imaginations, while still existing quite freely, would have to face the reality of competing directly with billions of others who also have passions and imaginations instead of using government policies to gain advantages.

I hope I've made my case for establishing a single world currency. Later in the book I want to visit immigration more deeply but until then, I want to start establishing the case for using energy as the basis for the single world currency. I want to eliminate as much of the seven consequences as possible while creating an economy which is closer to the seven golden rules where the price of Biryani in the USA is similar to the price of Biryani in Bangladesh.

Chapter 4
FAITH: TRIBULATION AND RAPTURE

You have probably seen the title for this chapter and are wondering what the Christian Tribulation and Rapture have to do with the establishment of a single world currency and related supporting systems. I ask, that if you have a moment, to do an internet search of the phrase "one world currency" and take a look at the descriptions for the first page of results. You should see what I have seen. The majority of results the search engines determine to be relevant to the subject all deal with the Christian "End Days" traditions. There are also a few results related to the International Monetary Fund (IMF) and the World Bank (WB). Given the United States has the world's largest economy, has hundreds of church denominations which originated in the United States, the teachings of Tribulation and Rapture as taught also originated in the United States, and these denominations have large influences in many developing countries as an extension of popular American culture, I feel it would be highly relevant to include a discussion on the matter as it relates to a single world currency.

The Tribulation and Rapture are associated with Christian "End Days" traditions which center on the second return of Jesus Christ. There are many variations in how these events play out, but there are usually some common events and characters at the focus of the traditions. These traditions are based mostly on the Book of Revelation, 1 Thessalonians, the Gospel of Matthew, the Book of Daniel, and the Book of Isaiah within the Bible.

The beginning of the story happened three days after the crucifixion of Jesus on the Roman cross per the request of the clergy whom opposed Jesus and on the reluctant authority of Pontius Pilate, the Roman governor of Judea. The body of Jesus had disappeared but his spirit was among his disciples, usually in an unrecognizable form. Finally, Jesus appeared in the body they recognized to solidify their faith in him and his teachings. After this, he left them and ascended to heaven. This event is known as the resurrection and was the foundation for Christian theology. Before Christ departed, he had promised that he would return again to fulfill the Jewish prophecies yet unfulfilled.

With the promise of Jesus returning, there have been many interpretations and insights as to how this will happen and what events will lead to the return, what will happen during the return, and how will the world be afterwards. I consider the pivot of these interpretations to be the Tribulation. The Tribulation is a period of time, often considered to be seven years, when there will be great destructive events occurring throughout the world where all mankind is affected. These events include great natural disasters and disasters brought on by man, such as war. Sometime before, during, or after the tribulation (there is interpretive variety here), the Rapture will occur. The Rapture is where those who truly believe in Jesus will meet Jesus up in the clouds in the air. These lucky people will face no more suffering and be eternally saved. No matter when the Rapture happens, after the Tribulation the Second Coming will happen. The Second Coming of Jesus will occur to defeat the forces of the singular Antichrist and bring peace upon earth and establish a kingdom in which Jesus is the sovereign King.

There are many varying stories as to who the Antichrist could be. Usually the figure is defined as being male, non-Christian, with a general thirst for power. Depending on what is going on in world affairs, this figure has been defined as being an atheist communist, a Nazi (although Christians were never targeted by Nazis solely for being Christian), Muslim, or even being a slick wealthy industrialist. The motivations of this character is to bring about the establishment of a one world government where Christians are persecuted and in general, the world devolves into a chaotic, sinful place where all that happens goes exactly in the opposite direction of the hopes and desires of Christians. What is interesting in this general story is a single world currency gets included with some of the institutions this Antichrist would implement.

Does this make me the Antichrist? Being a believer of God myself, I would certainly hope my ideas would not lead to the domination of evil and the suffering of mankind. Does this also mean I'm potentially speeding up the eventual return of Jesus? Being a believer of God, I guess that wouldn't be a bad thing but to be honest, I want the world to be a better place no matter what you believe in or don't believe in. Just in case, you the reader are concerned about the development of a single world currency as being an inherently evil thing, I would like the opportunity to ease your concerns. Please read on.

So far I have introduced this idea among my Christian friends and the general consensus is this is not a good idea because it would lead to the Antichrist. I admit, with the way monetary policy and economics is today, I totally understand your concerns. If we refer back to the seven consequences in Chapter 1, we see already the havoc the current system has brought on, a system operating with the assumed consent of Christians.

One of the first famous advocates of a single currency managed by a world central bank was the economist John Maynard Keynes. Keynes proposed this as a way to reduce the conflicting whims of national governments and felt this would bring about stability. The Great Depression had already destroyed much perceived wealth, created an increasingly impoverished population, and established the interconnectedness of a global economy where when one nation suffers, others will also suffer. One single currency would acknowledge these realities and start us on a new path of robust economy where growth can be sustained, wealth be generated, and jobs be had. The world governments did not heed Keynes advice but had instead created the WB and the IMF.

The WB and the IMF were designed to be multi-nation institutions whose purpose are to provide some type of stability in the worldwide economy as well as provide resources for the development of infrastructure and other projects which can benefit poorer nations and their people. One interesting aspect of these organizations is they are unelected bodies working in close coordination with private sector financial institutions, whose mission statements are profit-oriented. I will admit much of what these two institutions have accomplished provide positive benefits, but they have also received much criticism. Some of this criticism includes dictating how sovereign nations should govern themselves, the conflict of seeking financial gain in non-profit government projects, and picking and choosing projects based on a perceived political incentive system. I personally do not have an opinion on whether the good outweighs the bad, or vice versa, but I definitely believe these are institutions which can be improved upon. As they stand, unelected institutions working in conjunction with private entities who have created a system where the seven consequences are rampant, I could understand the reservations some people would have in granting even greater power and authority. A single currency managed by a single central bank, where no one is held accountable to any world citizens, without checks and balances, and only the passions and imaginations to lead their sciences and faith, would inherently lead to many trials and tribulations.

However, if in a belief system, things must go crazy bad before ultimate good could ever occur, wouldn't the believers of this system, such as Christians, be supportive of any path which could bring about the return of their Savior? Why be scared of what brings you hope? To me, it testifies to a lack of faith in those who express the most faith.

If an evil figure is evil for uniting people together, how would the rule of Jesus after His return be any different? Will people be united (an evil act associated with the Antichrist) or will there still be disunity and 180 different nations managing 180 different currencies?

If Jesus were to govern the world as King, how would the world economy look like? Would it remain as we currently know it or perhaps would he create a system which more closely follows the principles of religion, such as the seven golden rules from Chapter 2?

If Christians were to be in heaven as the second Jesus ruled the non-Christian world, who would listen to what he says, record what he says, act upon what he says, and peacefully be citizens to this kingdom? Does this mean there is a new religion, a new scripture, and new laws and principles to guide the people contemporary of this time? What would he teach and which non-Christians would be the first to help him?

I ask these questions because those who fear the consequences of a single world currency and potentially a governmental structure to support this endeavor have not fully questioned the consequences of what they claim to believe in. In their fear, the creation of unity is considered a bad thing, the development of an economic system where someone in Bangladesh can earn a similar wage to someone in the USA is considered unjust, and war is the only pathway towards peace. To me, this is twisted and goes against the very principles Jesus taught. These people who believe in tribulation and rapture end up preferring an unjust, greedy, war-mongering system instead of the equity, peace, and contentment promised to them.

I definitely agree a single world currency should not be managed as Keynes and other economists have suggested. This would bring about some short-term good to the world, but eventually lead to no checks and balances to the passions and imaginations of those who run this system. Any system which has such potential consequences needs to have checks and balances and accountability to elected institutions. I seek not a system of Antichrist, nor the system of today.

Perhaps there is a way where a single world currency can achieve all of the seven golden rules which multiple faith based organizations profess belief in and be acceptable to those who have no declared faith but share some humanist principles. In the next chapter, I want to start with a foundational principle to the single world currency, the foundations of which are God (no matter what name you call God) and that what is taught in the world scriptures and belief systems. This will require an active imagination, but an imagination whose journey is science and faith. Once this principle is established, maybe we can start some more economic scenarios or transactions, and discover a system which can be considered closer to that which Jesus (or any other manifestation of divinity) may find acceptable.

Chapter 5
FAITH AND SCIENCE: WHAT IS ENERGY?

This chapter will probably be the most complex subject I may have ever tried to write about. I'll continue to try to keep this as simple as possible, but I must warn that I may blow your mind. I do it to myself every single time I merge faith and science together in my mind. I will admit I'm far from any expert but I do invite you to take any ideas presented and go ahead and do further research. Investigate the truth and be inspired as you dig deeper and deeper into truth.

When reading about energy and the various types, I've never come across one singular definition of energy. This is because energy can be a wave, it can be a particle, it can be in action or it can be potentially in action. We eat energy, we see energy, when we touch another's skin we feel energy, basically every single action we take and every single imagination we have involves the use of energy in some way. We are alive because energy is within us in every single cell and all of our senses are used to experience energy in some form or another.

As we use technology to enhance our senses and use science to test what we observe, we are coming to better understandings of what energy is. Some of these understandings have led to three laws of energy as well as three laws of thermodynamics. We also have used faith, religion, and philosophy to also try to understand certain kinds of energies, such as figuring out the inner essence of ourselves, its purpose, and how to use these inner energies for positive outward change. I first want to start with the first law of energy. I'll try not to meander too much.

The first law of energy states energy can neither be created nor destroyed. Energy cannot be created from nothing and you can never lose energy. Energy must always exist, or in other words, energy is eternal. No matter how deeply we have observed energy, this has remained to be true. We observe in small systems, such as the human body, energy can enter but energy also is expended. Anything unused is stored for future use. This also works for the Earth. The sun provides the earth with constant energy and the Earth expends much of that energy as heat, reflections, etc. The Earth even stores some of the energy through organic processes such as plant photosynthesis and the eventual creation of hydrocarbons such as petroleum and coal. No matter how big of a system we have observed and no matter how small, this same law has remained true.

What else in our world is eternal, without loss or without gain? There are two things which I am familiar with at this time. The first has so far been able to be tested by science. This is mass and the law of conservation of mass. Mass, like energy, can have no loss nor gain, no matter how it is transformed by energy. The second thing has not been able to be tested through scientific means but is something people have theorized since we've been recording our own history. God. In every faith tradition, going back to aboriginal faith to modern day faith traditions and every point in between, there has always been an entity described as being eternal. So, for right now, we can say God is like energy and possibly like mass if we limit our definition of God as being eternal only.

How do we know energy is not mass or is not God? Let's start with mass. Mass is also hard to define but I would say mass is a property of a physical body and how much it can resist an energy input. I am about 83kg. A kg is a metric standard measurement of mass. We know if I am on a stable, flat surface, it can be hard to push me around unless you are quite musclebound and ripped. If you put me on a wheel and remain on the flat surface, you will notice I am much easier to push. My earth weight may be the same but my mass is actually less because I can resist your pushing less. If you try to push me up a hill on the wheel, it becomes very difficult again. My mass has increased. If you try to push me down a hill, you won't need much help at all and you may laugh as I pick up speed and crash into a hopefully soft object. In this case, I have little mass as I'm going downhill. What is interesting is as I pick up speed going downhill, I start to resist the energy again as I interact with the air. My mass starts to increase again and eventually, the rate of speed increase stabilizes.

In this simple scenario, we see mass can change depending on how various energies are applied. We also were interacting with gravity, which is also an effect of energy. Einstein had theorized when mass reaches higher speeds due to higher energy input, the mass also increases. Einstein suggested any mass which can achieve the speed of light would never age but it was impossible for mass to ever achieve this speed. So far there has been no evidence contrary. What this means is mass cannot be energy itself.

If a mass ages only because it cannot travel at the speed of light (or the speed of any electromagnetic (EM) wave), then it means light or any other EM wave must not age. Energy can be transformed but never age. Mass in its form can age, but will always exist in some form. Let's imagine something now. Say we have the light coming from the Sun. To us, it takes the light 8 minutes to reach us. This is an observation we make because we, confined in our mass, is moving so slowly that we observe this time. However, to the light waves emanating from the Sun, because it traveled at the speed of light, this energy did not age one bit. We aged 8 minutes but the light remained the same age. This also means then, if we are considering time, the light from its own perspective was both at the Sun and the Earth at the same exact time. Our mass may have moved in those 8 minutes, but we were never continuously in the same position during those 8 minutes, even if you were in a coma. Our bodies are constantly moving through space plus the Earth rotates.

If something can exist in multiple locations at the same time, does this mean the light is omnipresent? From our perspective, from our observations with our eyes and senses, it would not seem light is omnipresent. But from the perspective of light itself, if light had a perspective, it would seem to be everywhere at once. Now, we understand light interacts with mass, this is why we can see some colors reflected into our eyes and other colors are absorbed. The energy from the light, once it has interacted with mass, becomes transformed into other energy and either stored temporarily or immediately dispersed. Even when this energy transforms, it must still be in motion. We see this motion with atoms and their electrons, subatomic particles, and so on. No matter how deep our observation, we are able to observe this energy in motion. No matter the resulting effect of the energy, no matter how we observe it, from the perspective of the energy, it has never aged and it has been in every location without reference to time. I would assert energy is omnipresent.

Is there anything which shares the properties of being eternal and omnipresent? Mass has the properties of being eternal although with temporary forms, but can never be omnipresent due to its physical nature. This leaves one other entity, God. Through all the faiths I have had the opportunity of learning, God has been described as being omnipresent. That is, God has the ability to be anywhere and everywhere all at once. This maybe the human imagination at work, but it is intriguing how people in disconnected societies such as the Inca of Peru, the Hebrew of Egypt, the Hindu of Pakistan, and the Taoist of China had all similar imaginations of an entity which was eternal and omnipresent.

The second law of energy says energy always has a degree of disorder, which is when energy is transformed to a new state, you can never combine the new forms to recreate the old form. This is called entropy. The randomness of disconnected societies imagining a similar entity with such properties testifies that at least in a closed system called Earth, outside energy cannot lead to more disorder. For now, due to the Sun as the immediate source of energy, but also because all the universal energies are theoretically connected in space and time, we have achieved the opposite of disorder, called order.

This order is the result of energy in terms of science and this order is the result of God in terms of religion. I would like to say, for the sake of argument, energy is God and God is energy. I come to this conclusion after presenting the two properties of being eternal and omnipresent and later on in the book, I will further this argument as other topics arise. For now though, I will keep this chapter focused.

I am far from the first person who has made this type of link or claim, and there are even some quantum scientists who have developed a similar theory. For one possible explanation, I invite you to read about the Hamiltonian, which can be used to describe how kinetic and potential energies can exist independently of time. Also of interest is the Higgs boson, a particle which has been quite difficult to observe but could provide future answers as to how eternal energy first interacted with eternal mass. This particle has been called the God particle, although I'm not sure the particle itself would be God or perhaps the mode God interacts with the physical.

Now let's get back to the purpose of this book. This book is to imagine a single world currency whose economic system can get rid of the seven consequences and work within the seven golden rules. I would like to propose the foundation of this single world currency to be energy. Basing a currency away from precious metals, paper, or even simulated precious metals such as Bitcoin would allow a new paradigm to exist. This paradigm, if we can agree our scientific definitions for energy are at least similar to the traditional definitions of God, could allow us to evolve into an economic system where our transactions and method of calculations are based on God.

In the next chapter, I'm going to share the foundational principles of an energy based economy and energy based single world currency.

Chapter 6
ECONOMICS AND FINANCE: AN ENERGY BASED SINGLE WORLD CURRENCY

In the prior chapter, I introduced the foundational principle in using energy as the basis for a single world currency. To make reference to this concept more simply, I want to give this currency a name. The Ency.

Sometimes when we normally think of energy, often times the conversation focuses on electricity and fuel. I understand why as in business, the energy sector is defined this way. Due to this, we rarely think of other forms of energy as being energy. Being this way, anytime an energy based currency has been imagined or speculated, the focus is always on the business side aspect of industry. These forms of energy include petroleum, gas, coal, nuclear power, and renewable energies plus the value added components of these industries. However, despite this modern definition, the entire progression of human civilization had always required the use of other forms of energy.

When the first permanent settlements started to occur in areas such as modern day Mexico, Peru, Turkey, Syria, Pakistan, and China, the reason behind these permanent settlements was due to the ability to produce energy beyond the required needs of each person in the settlement. Before, how life worked was a person or people would need to hunt, fish, or gather enough food to meet their daily caloric needs. Some days these needs were met, other days they were not. When food was scarce, reproduction was low and probably death rates were higher. When food was abundant, reproduction could increase. You see, the very basic equation at this point was having enough energy to replace the energy used. If over a period of time the energy used by a person was more than they could eat, this person would starve and potentially die from hunger. The calorie as we call it today was the most basic form of energy human society was based upon.

Eventually technological advancements allowed various people to simultaneously develop agriculture. In Mexico corn and squash became staples, in Peru was quinoa, amaranth, and potatoes, in Turkey and Syria wheat and rye, in Pakistan sesame, and China rice and yams. I'm not saying these were the only foods, but these are foods which we know today have a lot of calories. Once a people were able to start producing more food than they needed to eat, we had a net benefit to society. You can also describe this phenomena as the people were producing more energy than they were consuming. Any society who has produced more energy than they consume have been able to store the energy for later use, such as grain bins or other storehouses, which could cover during times of natural disasters and to provide resources for trade. This extra energy was sometimes used in diplomacy, such as Egypt's relations with its ancient neighbors, or to help finance large construction projects such as early sanitation and monuments. Imagine all the food needed to feed the slaves/workers who built the pyramids in Egypt and Mexico for example. The surplus production of energy was the foundation of these great ancient civilizations.

Eventually civilizations, as technology progressed, discovered new ways to harness the energy. The Chinese were able to harness the energy flowing through water to develop their early textile and paper mills. Once this ability was harnessed, for a period of time the Chinese was one of the wealthiest societies, renowned for its economy, military, and sciences. In Europe, with the burning of coal and peat, steam was introduced as a way to empower steel. Industrial manufacturing and electricity generation soon followed. Europe quickly became a leader in economy, military, and sciences. This is of course a short statement on how civilizations have progressed, and I'm purposefully ignoring politics and the other human factors. Still, I strongly believe the course of civilizations throughout our history has been dependent on how much surplus energy we produce in relation to what we consume for our basic needs. This surplus energy can then be utilized increasingly for other purposes. Leonardo da Vinci never would have painted the Mona Lisa or drew plans of a helicopter if he was struggling to meet the energy demands his body required. Instead, because Italy was producing more energy than it could consume, da Vinci was able to harness some of this surplus energy as a fuel for the intellect. This intellect, another form of energy, helped encourage the further technological progress of civilization and perhaps mankind.

The purpose of recounting history from this perspective is to remind us not only of our humble beginnings, but also to the understanding energy is everywhere. The foundation of this energy is the calorie, also known as about 4.1 joules. Agriculture is the foundation of any society's ability to not only maintain themselves, but also to progress. However, in this modern age, those who produce agriculture are often among the world's most poor people unless directly subsidized by a government. Despite living in a supply and demand economy, we value our demand for food and their calories lower than any other industrial activity. Today though, I want to show how agriculture can be the basis of an economy which features the Ency.

When I demonstrated an example of the Chicken Biryani in the United States and Bangladesh, one thing I discussed was the price of rice, its production, and demand. Rice growing, at its essence, is solar energy being harnessed and transformed into something we can use. Plants are nature's way of harnessing all of this input. I was doing some research into how much rice can potentially be cultivated in the USA, I found a result of up to 6.8 million pounds per acre. After doing some math, this equates to about 12.8 million kWh (kilowatt hours) per acre. This is approximately 250 times the total electricity usage of an American home plus an average American vehicle. If you want to look at it another way, the rice yield is about 140 times of the per capita energy usage of all Americans to include their industrial and recreational activities. If this were looking at the average Bangladeshi, the rice yield at this rate would generate enough energy for 1940 people. People in Bangladesh use less energy than Americans do, although this may not necessary be good for economic growth in Bangladesh. To put things in perspective, I currently pay about $.1056 per kWh for electricity, making the rice yield per acre worth $1.3m. I digress however and focus on the point I would like to make in this chapter.

For now though, let's pretend all farmers in the world are living in equal situations. A farmer in rural Bangladesh produces the same volume of rice per acre as a farmer in rural California or Arkansas. Each farmer has the same amount of energy consumption and also has similar needs, such as eating full meals each day, living and maintaining adequate shelter, has fresh water, suitable clothing for the environment, and access to transportation to participate in commerce and social living. Wouldn't it make sense the energy produced by the farmer in the USA would be equal to the energy produced by the farmer in Bangladesh? Let us imagine an Ency is worth one kWh. The potential revenue for both farmers would be about 12.8 million Ency. Equal revenue without any price manipulations by governments, central banks, commodity traders, or anyone else. This would be the foundation of all economic activity, which is valuing life sustaining food and the people who grow it to a degree where none live in poverty.

Through this basic idea of this chapter, I strongly believe we are already working towards an economic system which brings us closer to the golden rules of economy and further away from the consequences. I understand agriculture is not the sole industry in the world, I am only saying it should be the foundation. I also understand not every country or local area is suitable for growing agriculture. Sometimes a land is able to but conditions change, such as when massive drought ravaged the rural areas of eastern Syria rendering land useless and virtually worthless. This systematically induced poverty created conflict which those who have worthy land is unwilling to help, due to the system at hand. Should land holding be a source of wealth for individuals, despite the consequences of natural disasters and climate change? I'm not ready to discuss these things yet, but as you can see, using an Ency as a single world currency does change how we calculate things.

In the next chapter, I want to further break down agriculture through all levels of society, starting first and foremost the family unit, the most personal organization of justice and economy we experience in our lives.

Chapter 7
FAMILY: A UNIT OF GOVERNMENT AND ECONOMY

This chapter, I would like to introduce a simple observation I have made and the significance it has upon all systems of economy and governance mankind has ever devised. The family is the foundational structure of government and economics. In many cultures throughout the world, many of the decisions an individual makes is in direct relation to its impact on the family, even if this person is single and without children. Marriage, employment, distribution of wealth, faith, relations with neighbors, living location, educational attainment, and even leisure are all parts of the decisions families may make. I also state the forms of justice, such as reward and punishment, the forces of freedom and oppression, and even equality and inequality all start with the family. Noting this, I feel any economic system and government structure should acknowledge the importance of the family.

I want to share a few stories in how this dynamic sometimes plays out in the world. I have a close female friend in Pakistan who is well-educated and in a middle-class family. We had met, in all places, on an online forum where we discussed the role of women in a religious society, with specifics on establishing equality. She had originally believed she should be the one to determine important matters such as who she will marry, where she will live, and what career she will seek. The immediate family was supportive of the education and the extended family felt she should focus more on marriage and being more traditional. After some years though, there was increasing pressure upon her with little support in her career goals. Finally, she accepted an engagement invitation to a man she hadn't met, but in a location she had at least hoped to live in. This friend has taken ownership of this decision and seems to be happy, but this was a decision made mostly with the consideration of the family.

In this above example, there is no way to predict how the future will be. It could turn out she could end up living a very happy and fulfilling life because the family, as a group with many experiences, knew what was best for a young individual with less experience. She could end up being unhappy because her original goals and dreams had to be altered or sacrificed due to the will of the majority. To some outside the situation, there are a few ways to think about what kind of government this was and its repercussions.

One way to think of this is a democratic government, where each person had their say. There is a legislature who recommends the law, and perhaps the parents or elders execute the law. There is no judicial structure. There is also no constitution which defines the rights of all members within the family. In this case, the majority does rule although there is potential for causing oppression among individual members. Oppression, as I would define it, is a combination of treating someone (or a group) in an unfair way or the threat of some type of harm if a certain way is not followed. In this case, my friend was regularly reminded she could not possibly be happy on another path and must choose this path to bring herself happiness as well as respect to the rest of the family. Even if this is not oppression, it is at least pressure which can cause worry. In a greater society, when we examine the country of Pakistan at large, we see a country who struggles with their democratic institutions. At once there is rule of the majority but also constant conflict and struggle among various minorities due to oppressive behaviors by the majority. Due to this, Pakistan is regularly considered a near-failed nation with a government which is barely able to exercise power throughout its sovereign lands.

Another way to think about this family is this of an oligarchy, a government which is controlled by a minority. Often times an oligarchy has the appearance of a democracy, other times it can seem autocratic, but no matter how it is formally structured, only a few have power. In this case, those with the greatest influence are the parents or other elders who expect a higher degree of respect and influence due to their station of parent and elder. In this case, we have a person who had little voice due to the structure and expectations set up by few who wielded the power. In this case, one may resist but it can come with clear consequences if the oligarchy is directly challenged. In Pakistan within the greater society, it has often occurred commanders within the military have wielded the highest degree of influence in politics and business. When these commanders are challenged, sometimes there are violent acts in response. Mind you, I believe most countries have an oligarchy structure but to varying degrees.

The purpose of this first story is at least to help imagine the consequence of how higher levels of government end up reflecting the average family structures. How we choose to organize ourselves within a family influences our expectations throughout the rest of our political organizations.

Another story I would like to share is of another friend from the Philippines who is now working in Dubai. As many in the world may know, the phenomena of Filipino overseas workers is very common in countries with a need for less expensive labor. This is due to a combination of factors where individuals realize there are better opportunities for higher pay outside of the Philippines in countries such as Hong Kong, Taiwan, the United Arab Emirates, Saudi Arabia, and Australia. With my friend, this decision to work in Dubai was not solely her own decision. There is a high degree of pressure for a young person out of high school to start providing for the needs of siblings and the parents. There are no governmental institutions such as social welfare or retirement financial vehicles to assist aging citizens. As wages in the Philippines stay low, much due to similar factors as in the example of Bangladesh in Chapter 2, the ability for a young person to provide support for aging parents, siblings, and themselves is nearly impossible. I guess part of this is a desired quality of life beyond what they already experience, early retirement as compared to many western countries, and larger family sizes. To meet these needs, a young person often feels there is no other choice but to work overseas, a decision which has become a cultural norm. After a long decision making process, my friend applied to be an au pair in Dubai, a job which requires no formal education but pays more than a job she could get in the Philippines using her formal education. She did not want to live in Dubai as the culture and environment is fundamentally different than in the Philippines, but now she is able to provide for the family.

This story reflects how a family, when taken together, can be defined as a collective economic entity. The resources of many are redistributed to meet the needs of all. I will not discuss this decision with the lens of governance but solely through one of economics and finance. As structured, the family faces many tough decisions to achieve a certain quality of life for each of its members. There is an expectation the children should repay their parents for the sacrifices the parents made in raising the children, and this repayment is often in the form of sacrifice by the children. On the good side, the aging live a simple life if they desire with food, shelter, and involvement with the family. On the bad side, the younger members sometimes have to delay having their own family, a decision their parents may not have made a generation earlier.

You see, as income inequality throughout the world increases due to various reasons, the ability for families to meet their needs becomes more and more difficult. The income potential often does not keep up with the cost structures imposed. Still, the family themselves decides what the quality of life is for each of them. If one member is able to earn significantly more than another, there is an expectation that one member can provide more to the rest of the family. This is similar to a progressive tax structure. The one member has not lost their incentive to work but instead has a greater incentive to continue increasing their income because they know they can not only profit themselves, but that of the greater whole.

What type of quality of life is suitable for a family and its individual members? This could be one which is up to debate, but I would suggest at least one where there is no chance of hunger, there is shelter which is suitable in protecting any personal belongings, enough fresh clothing to meet the needs of the culture and work, and enough land to produce a potential surplus of energy. This latter portion, enough land to produce a potential surplus of energy, could be controversial.

The majority of the world has so far implemented a system which recognizes the right to private ownership of land. I believe if this is an agreed upon right by the majority of a population, then this right cannot be deprived and the greater society should meet the needs of allowing access in the exercising of this right. This would mean then, a certain minimum amount of tax-free land, to be owned or used by an average size family of that population. If the majority truly do not believe in this right to private ownership of land by taking actions which reduce the ability of the majority to own land, such as through implementing a tax code which discourages poor individuals from ownership or supply and demand price structures which create prices well beyond the means of the poor, then this right to ownership of land should be revoked for all members of the society, whereupon ownership is communal, not individual.

My final story in this chapter will involve my own personal experiences with relationships. This involves discussions, consultations, and even negotiations with an outside family, not my own. At varying points throughout my life, certain relationships had been discouraged by either my family or another's family. Some issues I experienced within my own family included dating a woman who was a minority in my society, one of African descent. This was looked down upon my family. I was told it is permissible to be friends, but not permissible to be lovers or worse, married. The eldest members of my family, and some younger, believed those of African descent were inferior to me, a western European descendent. At another instance a relationship was discouraged because she was Pentecostal and the eldest members of my family preferred someone from a more traditional Protestant faith, such as a Lutheran. With other families, a relationship was discouraged with me due to me being a white American instead of being a Cuban, or I would only be accepted if I convert to another faith.

With these examples, we see how the family, as a unit of diplomacy, can try to influence interfamily affairs through soft-power and in extreme cases like honor killings, hard-power. The consequences of these diplomatic relations can include changing beliefs, reinforcing stereotypes, or as what often happens in modern families throughout the world, treating others as inferior on the basis of skin color, national origin, belief system, ethnic identity, income attainment, and even just the perception of these classes.

For right or wrong, for better and for worse, the family is the integral base of governance for most of us. Sure, I acknowledge there are many families who do not function as a structured entity. I will even admit right now, my family does not function this way but because of this, the individual members have a limited support structure, both financially and emotionally. For a majority of people however, there is a resemblance of a family as being a political and governmental unit, an economic bloc, and diplomatic unit. A family exercises sovereignty where it can and when needed, families come together to potentially enhance their positions.

To conclude this chapter, I want to start thinking about the prior chapter and this one, where the foundation of the Ency based economy can interact with this foundation of the family unit. To me, the family is the most important unit in the world, one which needs to be encouraged and protected. Any change, such as a radical concept of the Ency, can only be effective if it can demonstratively improve the conditions of the sovereign family unit, whether this family is in Pakistan, the Philippines, the United States, or anywhere. In a globalized economy and political structure, what happens to one family can directly or indirectly have effect on the other. In a way, all families are thus connected as a complex singular unit called mankind. If this improving condition for all families can come through a lens of justice for all due to the adherence of the seven golden rules of economy, then this should, as a natural result, improve the quality of life each of the individual families which constitute the larger family of mankind.

Chapter 8
ECONOMICS: MINIMUM INCOME AND TAXATION

I want to close the writings regarding agriculture and family by putting the last few chapters together. As I view agriculture the foundation of economic activity and the family as the foundation of government, I would like to at least propose how these two could be organized under the Ency currency.

The first thought is to imagine the needs of a family. What does a family need? What is the quality of life every person should have? For now, I witness differing expectations of an individual evaluating what their quality of life should be versus the quality of life for their neighbors, no matter if those neighbors are immediately next to them, in another community, or even in another country. For as long as there is conflict between what "I need" and what "they need," this will always only be a philosophical question without an answer. However, if there could be some type of consultation as to what a basic quality of life should be, then I am highly supportive.

I personally believe it starts with whatever human rights we have collectively described and agreed upon, such as with the United Nations Declaration of Human Rights. Sometimes I feel these declarations are more altruistic than real, especially when considering how we choose to organize ourselves, or how we consent to our organization, despite expressing certain ideals. For example, in the last chapter we see how we can have a democracy whose government expresses the freedom of speech, but we may accept to organize ourselves into families or even corporations where this freedom is replaced with censorship. Human rights must exist at every level of society which enforces some kind of legal or judicial system. If not, then nations can never fully be the bearers of ideals the smaller organizations go against. I say this because our smallest units of organization, such as that of a family, religious organization, business, etc. are far more representative of us (all of the I's and they's) than a distant national government could ever be.

My first rule then, for the organization of agriculture and family, is that a family be defined as the smallest level of government. This is where organizational rules are first formed, where we recognize leaders, where we experience reward and punishment which are the foundations of all justice, and where we experience consultation, conflict, and a political process. In my head, I've theorized about a nuclear family having a small constitution, but honestly it isn't required. I feel the recognition is the most important part at this point, as this is a radical departure from the majority view. If a family does not want to be recognized as a mode of government, then the powers of justice have to be rescinded and delegated to the next highest organization. This could be a village for example, or if the family prefers their local religious institution. I think it is perfectly acceptable to be able to "opt-in" or "opt-out" in your most representative form of government. I believe in consent to governance. I'll describe another time what higher levels of government will be. In the meantime, the family decides the roles each member has.

The family in an agricultural area falls under a village government. The village government has certain powers and responsibilities to the families and religious institutions within its boundaries. Here, the members serving in the village are elected directly by the families and must have a written constitution defining the roles of the village government, and the rights of the families and individuals of the village. The most important question the village government must answer is "What is the quality of life we desire for all village members?" For now, I will say economically or materially, every family should have a right to shelter, food, water, suitable clothing for the environment, education, electricity, and access to transportation networks. Others within the actual village may make other decisions, but for the sake of this book, I will define the basic needs as this.

Not every person in the village will be farmers and of course there will be other businesses and varying levels of trade and commerce going on. Still, producing food is the most important activity. How much food should a person be entitled to? The United States Department of Agriculture has defined the caloric needs of a person depending on age, gender, and activity level. For now, I will use their recommendation for a 16-18 year old active male for each person, as this is the maximum. The USDA says 3,200 calories are needed per day, or 3.72 Ency. This would amount to 1,357 Ency per year. The average household size in the world varies but according to the United Nations, a household in Burkina Faso is nearly 6 people or 2.1 in Germany at the lowest. In Burkina Faso, maybe the village may use 6 people in their calculation of the family size, bringing the total Ency to

8,146.

How much shelter should a person have? Should there be limits on square meters, the number of bedrooms, or other factors? I think more should be envisioned as to how much land an average family would require to produce the Ency needed for their food, and any food produced to provide the materials for shelter, the maintenance of shelter, clothing, electricity, and so forth. Whatever the energy is required to produce those items will need to be added into this minimum. As of now, I do not know these values but given the advancement of science, we do have the capability to understand how much energy goes into the production of every good and service, plus any extra value we add due to the transforming effect of the intellect.

Once this minimum is established, we now have a basis for all other economic activity. Any individual, family, business, etc. must be held to this minimum standard. What if a family is unable to meet the minimum Ency requirements? Then the rest of the village must provide the difference. What if a family is able to produce more than the minimum? Then I would recommend the village include a progressive taxation system. I feel where possible, taxes should be as low as possible to meet the needs of the village while allowing the incentive to earn higher income through innovation and improvements. Reward those who are successful while ensuring those who are less successful have their basic common needs met.

What about the individual who has moved or has no family ties in the village? Their basic needs should be the same as that of the family, even if their household is only the one person. The person should be encouraged in providing enough in case this individual is wanting to start a family.

What about the disabled individuals in the village? If a person is unable to work or provide for their basic needs, the village needs to provide those needs. If the disabled individual is a member of a family, the family must provide for their needs with assistance from the village.

What about the elderly? Every able bodied and able minded individual should contribute to the family. Sometimes, such as even in motherhood, work may not directly contribute to the daily production of Ency, but we understand they still provide value. This value could maybe come through the future transformation of energy, or future investment of Ency. Still, if an elderly person comes to the point in their life they are unable to contribute, they must still be taken care of.

One of my biggest criticisms of a capitalistic focused economy is we most often value the new more than the old. When a new technology comes out, we desire the new and discard the old when we can. This happens with manufactured goods, clothes, and unfortunately this also happens with people. Sometimes we value the life of the unborn or newly born much more than those who have lived awhile. This could be because we understand the potential future ability to transform energy is greater with the unborn and youth when compared to an 80 year old, but we also neglect to understand the value one can still provide, or the responsibilities we have to those entrusted to us. Many times the elderly are discarded from a home into a nursing center or are emotionally abused and neglected for no longer being able bodied or able minded. Any humane, ethical society must take care of their elderly.

This village, with taxation and directly representing the goals and aspirations of all members in the village, will save what it can for future needs while also providing the basic services the society desires, such as transportation networks, education networks, utilities, and legal services. They will protect and provide for the rights defined and empower their people to determine their modes of being while ensuring the exercising of these rights do not impair another's ability to exercise these rights.

What about property tax? There should be no property tax for the minimal required land to meet the needs of the people. If a property tax is instituted, although it is not required, then this should be progressive as well. The more land an individual, family, or organization uses beyond the minimum, the higher the tax should be. This will discourage wasteful uses of land although still providing the ability for capitalists to organize large amounts of land to production.

The village will work with other nearby jurisdictions, and any government in echelons above, to also meet those needs. The echelons above cannot directly tax the village's people as they cannot be directly represented, but the echelon above does represent the village and the government formed in the village. More will be defined later in the book about the layers of government, but no matter what, the village is the cornerstone.

For the final question, what about a city? The city, to me, is a collection of neighborhoods, or a collection of villages which are interconnected. Being this way, they should be treated this way. No matter how urban or rural a village is, the families and individuals of the village determine the minimum basic needs and requirements. There may be little agriculture in certain villages if they are urban. Despite this phenomena, the minimum needs can still be determined by the people.

The idea behind all of this is the needs and expectations of a people, in any given point in time, could be different and variable. Big government, such as a federal government, does not determine this minimum quality of life but you do. The people closest to you do. This may make our reliance on others seem stronger, and depending on your perspective this can be good or bad. The reality is, we have always been reliant on others in every mode of living, even indirectly. Even an individual living independently, providing all their needs on their own, was at some point reliant upon the intellectual endeavors of those this individual learned from. There is an illusion of independence, but the reality is mankind has always been interdependent on others for sustenance and any improvements in civilization. The village and the families empowered can use this interconnectedness to help each other, even as some compete with each other. Knock a person down with one hand but help them on their feet with the other. I want all to end up on their feet, no matter how hard they fell.

So far, with the introduction of the Ency and the village family based economy and government, we can start going closer to the golden rules from Chapter 2. We still accept the use of money, a money based on the reality of energy and God. We have an acceptance and encouragement on working. One can work to profit themselves but there is a built in system of shared goals and aspirations which can naturally replace common modes of charity with the idea we value each other as equals. The members of the villages and families may determine how to provide the needs of those in need solely by being required to understand their own basic needs. The "I" has been applied to the "they" in equal measure. Usury so far has not been eliminated but I imagine each village could determine and define what usury is and what would be acceptable interest rates if any borrowing needs to happen. Still, they would be mindful the village has to provide the minimum needs and could understand the hazards of creating interest rates or borrowing rules which could require a village member to later need village assistance to meet their needs. I find it silly in today's economic paradigm, we find it ok to charge someone up to 25% interest to borrow money for a few weeks and then blame the person for remaining in poverty, unable to negotiate better interest rates, and require social welfare programs to be sustained. I think this is a ridiculous outcome and should never happen.

Moderation would be required to exist, unless of course the entire village feels it is alright for everyone to either be destitute of any material wealth or that each person is entitled to more wealth than the wealthiest member. Then we have a problem. I just feel placing yourself in another's shoes creates moderation in our relations with others although I do understand moderation in our desires and wants can be difficult. Having the Ency be energy based still encourages the village to perform their calculations with not only their material and physical wants, but also their abilities to produce, transform, and use energy, an energy which can be considered spiritual. We have not introduced debt yet, about it being a promise or anything which governs debt, but this can be addressed soon.

At this point, however, I feel we have a solid starting point in the organization of society to support the usage of the Ency.

Chapter 9
ECONOMICS: INTRODUCTION TO INTELLECTUAL PROPERTY

A few instances so far in this book, I've mentioned the abilities or potentials of energy transformation. Energy transformation is any process in which energy is used to change the properties or essence of matter or other energies. The initial input leads to a new output. This output should, hopefully, bring added benefit of some form otherwise the entire process is wasteful.

There are many recognized modes of energy transformation most people are familiar with, such as with electricity generation, body metabolism, or how fire interacts with various objects. However, one of the most important modes of energy transformation we interact with is the human intellect. The intellect, or as many prefer to say "our understanding" of various things is often the very catalyst for change. The intellect has been involved in the selective breeding programs ancient Mexicans used to develop maize (corn), the technologies and methodologies of both war and peace, our modes of government, our forms of faith, and basically everything in between.

As of now scientists and doctors continue to unravel the mysteries which involve the intellect. So far we know the intellect involves energy's interactions with the brain cells (neurons), which surprisingly causes nearly infinite numbers of results. We experience these varied results when you can have twins who experience nearly identical upbringings in identical environments, but still have varied personalities and character traits. In a way, the output is as unique as a person's fingerprint or iris. This has been a mystery ever sense the earliest philosophers had asked "Who am I?" while always never answering "I am this other person."

How the intellect effects economy is quite profound, and in a way, impossible to fully capture with data. Infinite variables creates impossible computation and the best we can do is remove variables to gain inferences or correlations in a near vacuum. The intellect is both real but elusively like a mirage. In the study of economics, often times it is taught by using equations whose multipliers include technology, capital, labor, and this unidentifiable quality. Needless to say these equations only work if this unidentifiable quantity is assumed, which can never result in a fully accurate calculation. This unidentifiable quality could be as simple as luck, as many times there appears to be randomness in all results. This quality could be the intellect, although the intellect also factors into how tech, capital, and labor are all used. It could be both a mix of luck and intellect. The thing is, no one truly knows and if the answer really is luck and intellect, we have yet the capabilities to identify or measure them.

You may read this and say, Josh, we can measure the intellect. We have IQ tests and other standardized tests which measure intelligence. This is true, but an IQ test is also only in a vacuum. This is a measure of isolated measures, not the potentials or effects of the intellect as it interacts with the world's wants and needs. The intellect within economy requires experts in psychology and other behavioral sciences, mathematicians, economists, and others in many other fields. Once again, I admit I am not an expert in any of these fields, but am presenting ideas as I've observed and putting them in a way which I hope could be tried and tested.

The intellect, even in the modern day, has been a difficult subject to tackle in regards to its usage in our economy. Maybe the most common usage of the word intellect is when we discuss intellectual property. These two words together seem to create an idea there are things of the intellect which can be owned, which thus can be controlled, traded, and sold. The most common forms of intellectual property we interact with are usually associated with the arts, such as music, books, movies, software, and the designs of commonly used products. Intellectual property can also include methodologies of performing a task or work, and in some rare cases, discoveries one makes about nature such as when Monsanto was able to patent a specific gene used in its seeds.

As society has defined these certain kinds of intellectual items as property, we have established legal principles which helps manage their usage. We have created patents which grant an inventor sole rights of an intellectual property for a certain amount of years, copyrights which grants a creator of content sole rights to the production and distribution of the content, and trademarks which grants an individual or corporation sole rights to a marketing concept. As with currencies, each government has different laws regulating intellectual properties and some governments do not recognize or enforce another country's intellectual property laws. Much of these differences in defining intellectual property and rights associated with them has many effects and consequences.

IP Consequence #1: The price or value of a specific intellectual property type could vary from country to country. An example would be the price of an MP3 on the Apple iTunes store. In India, the prices for a popular song is approximately $.20 while in the USA, the price is $1.19.

IP Consequence #2: There is inefficient markets involved in the trade of intellectual property. The biggest inefficiency is the lack of a clear mode of price discovery, where information is obtained by buyers and sellers as to the real price of an item for a near period of time.

IP Consequence #3: The potential benefits of intellectual property are limited through the establishment of IP monopolies or the denial of intellectual property due to political purposes. Monopolies are created when only one person or company has sole rights to the IP, thus eliminating competition using that particular IP. Political parties may create rules to limit IPs due to conflict with party ideals or a perceived threat to the party themselves.

Unfortunately, any given IP could suffer from all three consequences, especially if the intellectual property seems disruptive to an older technology, tradition, or idea. How many countries have governments and corporations which practice censorship, or have rules in place which make it extremely difficult to invent and innovate?

If a person desires to live in a truly free market but lives in a country where these three consequences exist, once again as with currencies, you do not experience a free market. You experience a system which limits the potentials of a free market solely to protect certain individual's interests. If you've ever heard the phrase "information is power" then you understand why intellectual property is managed and regulated in the manner it is. As in the United States, intellectual property is a right for all to pursue, but whose power only a few is allowed to wield.

In order for any economy to function most smoothly, like the movement of products and services across the world, the movement of intellectual property is required to continue the development of society into a more ordered and peaceful state. This is due to the effect the intellect has, the effect of energy transformation. Like a nuclear reaction, one transformation leads to another transformation, creating a chain of reactions which continue having greater effect upon those within its grasp. Unlike a hydrogen bomb or a nuclear power plant, the fuel behind the intellect is infinite, thus the chain reaction can continue on endlessly if given free reign. I hope in the world of the Ency, we can reevaluate how the intellect interacts with our economy and see if we can find a more just system where the three IP consequences are eliminated or reduced while still allowing for innovation.

The key to the entire discussion about intellectual property is as follows: Can the intellect be a property? If so, how can its ownership be managed? If not, how does this change our current modes of regulating the intellect?

In the next chapter, much like I did with the energy portion, I want to dig into a scientific and theological topic of what the intellect truly is. I believe understanding this foundation can help point us in a proper direction in understanding how the intellect, and its energy transformations, should function in an Ency based economy.

Chapter 10
FAITH AND SCIENCE: THE INTELLECT

The intellect is one of the mysterious forces of our existence, both as it relates to our individual selves and as to its effects throughout all of creation. So far, what we know about the human intellect is there is a relationship between our neurons and the energy interacting with the neurons. A neuron is a special cell in the body which is energy excitable, meaning it reacts to various charges from electricity. The type of reaction depends on the individual cell, which can have its own composition of water and other elements, such as potassium and sodium. We have neurons in the brain, spinal cord, nerves, eyes, ears, muscles, and every pathway in between. Even the heart, a large muscle functioning on electrical pulses, relies on neurons to work properly.

Neurons themselves are complex. In the human body, there are hundreds of kinds and each are alive. Each have a nucleus, which stores their DNA and information from elsewhere, such as the brain or other neurons. This DNA and information are much like the potentialities and realities each neuron is capable of. Neurons are long-lived, but they also die and new ones are created at a rate so far undetermined by scientists.

Holistically, we can say the neurons are the foundation of this electromagnetic reality which interacts with our primary senses and provides us with consciousness, awareness, free will, and intelligence. Any thought or action requires activity by the neurons. Without proper function of these neurons, we start to lose our capabilities, such as with Alzheimer's, Parkinson's, or even concussions. The way electricity interacts with each cell's unique composition (which creates a unique person) helps determine our personalities, feelings, and all of these inward attributes we develop and hold important. Values such as trustworthiness, loyalty, moderation, kindness, and etc. each are manifested within each neuron's potentials and capabilities as well as the potentials and capabilities of the entire neural network.

An interesting observation I remember making while in high school is how fast information can travel between two people. For example, like many guys I was highly interested in the women of my school. Occasionally, one would even express interest in me. Sometimes there would be a glance, a shy expression, or even a warm smile we would share. When a woman smiles at you, immediately you feel it. This feeling does not happen one second later but instantaneously. She smiles and I get the warm fuzzies. My heart rate may increase slightly and I instantly make a reacting decision based on many factors, but whose factors I am able to sort through and process instantly. I may return the smile, I may look a different direction shyly, I may look around to see if any of my buddies notice, or I may have already imagined our wedding. It is extremely crazy how fast we are able to process information. This smile, for all intents and purposes, traveled to me at the speed of light. The smile came to me through energy waves and photons, came into contact with me, and not only did my eyes respond but so did the rest of my body. A smile isn't just a visual observation, but it is an outward expression of an inner energy. She projected a feeling and thought which existed from within her and made me feel it from within myself, in an instant.

See, we know how electromagnetic waves can be used to store human created information. My favorite songs on the radio, my favorite comedies on TV, and connections through social media are all testimonies to our awareness and abilities to use electromagnetic waves (radio, light) to transmit complex data. The smile a girl deploys my way also uses this same technology. It came to me with the right frequency, the right amplitude, and the right resonance. In this case, our neurons at that moment were sharing the same energy, the same information, and in a true sense, they were connected. She and I were connected, all through a smile across a classroom.

The human intellect experiences at a near constant rate, stimuli from the energies around us. The sounds of music and traffic, the sights of flowers and concrete, the touch of a cool breeze and warm sunlight, the smells of chocolate chip cookies and expended fuel, and the taste of cool mints and apples are all examples of these energies we are bombarded with. Each individual stimuli interacts with a neuron which causes a chain reaction within the entire network. The energy is flowing, but uniquely flowing depending on the composition of the cells and the total composition of the network. The experiences we feel, even if a person next to use experiences the same thing, has unique results for each person experiencing. When a bullet goes off, one may duck, one may stand with tremors, another may jump in front of another, or one may attempt to fire a bullet of their own. Each outcome is completely natural and demonstrative of the variations energy has within our bodies.

This intellect has memory. This memory can take the form of existing within a specific neuron, but always at the ready with an awaiting electrical charge. In the dream state, our neurons are projecting a new reality comprised of this stored information and even somehow able to create new memories. No matter what level of reality we are aware of, we are simultaneously interacting with the energies of all realities. This has amazing consequences for the potential evolution of mankind, although I want to go to another direction.

In the laws of the conservation of energy, one of the laws discusses entropy. In any closed system, anytime energy is expended in one form that energy transforms into a form which is more disordered. For example, when I burn my favorite scented candle, I understand in an hour, there will be more smell and heat but less wax. Eventually, my candle will have no more wax and no matter how hard I try, I cannot combine the smell, smoke, and heat back into a candle. The energy is still out there somewhere, but in a less orderly and usable state. However, the laws of entropy only work in an entirely closed system. What system is there which is entirely closed? We've not been able to identify this, or at least prove with a mathematical certainty the existence of a closed system. What about the Sun? It has the Milky Way galaxy? What about the Milky Way? It has the Universe. What about the Universe? It potentially is part of another greater whole. Reality, no matter how far we zoom in or zoom out, it is more like a fractal with repeating patterns. Look at an atom and see the nucleus having electrons orbiting it. Look at the moon and observe it orbits our Earth. Creation, as far as we know, repeats itself in degrees, in scope, and in scale.

What does entropy have to do with intelligence? I believe, with the evidences existing in both faith and science, intelligence is the ultimate outside source which keeps disorder from dominating our creation. That is, intelligence is the ordering factor. We can witness how, to many varying degrees, how the human intelligence has transformed the environment and improved the quality of life of many through the arts and sciences. I'm not ignoring negative impacts of technology, but acknowledging there are many good things which have come. The application of the intellect has ordered our society more than it has disordered. We also see how from seemingly nothing, the solar system and the galaxies had become ordered. The general consensus theory is eventually all of this will cease to exist, but perhaps it will lead to a more ordered state. Let me share some potential stories as to why.

The first will be a simple observation about an adopted puppy. This puppy was taken away from its mother nearly immediately upon birth due to troubles giving birth. He was raised by my friend and was my friend's first dog. This puppy immediately recognized my friend, and other people, as having the ability to provide for its needs. This puppy also expressed its gratitude much like dogs often do, with licks and tail wags. This puppy did not learn this from its mother nor from us. Somehow, this puppy already had this information. Later on, once it started to grow up, he came across his first dog, which looked nothing like him. Without being told, this dog immediately was aware this creature was like himself, and they proceeded to sniff each other's butts and cautiously get to know each other. Once again, this was not taught from my friend nor by his mother. The puppy just knew. Finally, one day walking around a nearby forested area, we came across a small snake. The puppy, now a year old, without any commands approached the snake and with swiftness and precision, avoided the snake's bite and clamped down on the snakes neck. The dog, without any teaching, recognized the snake as a threat to himself and to us and knew exactly how to incapacitate the snake.

Many have described such knowledge as innate or instinctive. The ancient philosophers such as Plato had viewed innate knowledge as being imparted upon us by God or some other spiritual being with an intellect. As science has progressed, those such as Chomsky came to the conclusion this phenomenon is purely a product of our biology, our DNA, and exists as genetically programmed information which all of the same genetic types share. This means the puppy either had awareness of other dogs due to God or because of its shared DNA with other dogs. Both conclusions could potentially be correct, so I wouldn't rule them out. No matter the origin of innate knowledge, it cannot be denied it exists and that the knowledge in both scenarios come from sources which do not originate from the puppy. Even the DNA came from his mommy and daddy and not himself.

Another story could be like that which is common in the religious histories. There are some stories which describe the founders of our modern faiths to have been born with certain innate qualities. The Buddha, for example, upon birth had pointed to the sky and said he is ".the most venerable teacher of Gods and men." As a child he was described as compassionate and highly meditative, with wisdom beyond his years. He taught things no one else had taught and had knowledge no teacher had given. Jesus is described as teaching as a young boy in the Jewish Temple and imparting knowledge no one could have taught. Similar stories exist with Krishna, Muhammad, and the Bab. The result of this innate knowledge resulted in religious movements which still have effect in this world, inspiring millions and in some cases, billions, to try to learn from these bearers of knowledge.

Was the wisdom these historical figures were born with a product of DNA, potentialities existing in all of mankind, or were they provided this knowledge from a source of divinity? Some say these stories are but fictional myths, but in the case of the Bab, these stories were documented by historians in Iran in the early to mid-1800, and observed by outsiders of many nations. I prefer to go by this idea, if someone has imagined it or believed it, a portion must be true. What I can definitely testify to is the ordering influence each of these people had to their immediate societies. After Muhammad was the start of an Islamic Golden Age where Arabia and later Syria were the pinnacles of civilization, the pinnacles of order. This all came from an origin where Arabia was fractured and disordered to the point little history or influence remains in the present day. From disorder came order.

Information then, the inputs and outputs of the intellect then, can exist before and after our neurons have processed this information. The ideas of Plato, even though he has passed away over 2,000 years ago still exist among us, being the foundations of more complex knowledge or in some instances, still be the source of knowledge. Whether the intellectual output is stored and transmitted orally or written, it exists. Jesus, a bearer of innate knowledge stated "my words shall not pass away." Evidence would show this to be true and should potentially be true in the future. Even if mankind annihilates itself, a potential future intelligent life form could eventually access those very words of Jesus.

Look at the images of the Hubble Telescope if you have time. When the images of distant celestial bodies are captured, astronomers often state something like "10 million years ago" or any real time in the past, this was how the celestial body looked. To us, this is an ancient knowledge we are receiving. We are receiving information from stars, black holes, and quasars whose information originated billions of year ago from our perspective. In Chapter 5, I described how all energy is infinite, a concept undisputed in science. This means the electromagnetic realities we discover, no matter how far away, is infinite. The information provided to us is timeless and ageless. The information is not 10 million years old from the perspective of the energy and information. Information and the intellect then, is also infinite and never ages. Age of information is purely relative, meaning age only exists because this is the only way we can observe information for now.

This same energy the Hubble Telescope observes interacts with us, even without the aid of the telescope. It may be weak, much like when a car moves beyond its ability to receive my favorite FM radio station, but it still exists. I'm not saying this is astrology, but the infinite energies of billions of years ago still have information which comes into contact with our senses, comes into contact with our neurons. What comes from our neurons also has the potential to go right back to those ancient stars and affect them. This is reality.

What levels of existence can have intellect? I believe all levels, according to their capacities, have varying potentials to carry, process, and transmit information. We see how a tree responds to decreasing light and colder temperatures. The tree processes the information and tells itself to start entering a hibernation where the majority of its energy moves underground. We see how a caterpillar will cocoon itself for its future metamorphosis. We see even how hydrogen just does not randomly bind itself to any available element with an available charge. It seems to choose what form it will take. No matter how deeply you zoom into creation, the atoms, subatomic materials, and even the neutrinos, being bearers of energy, are also the bearers of information and intellect. No matter how far you zoom out, the planets and other celestial bodies also bear information and intellect. In a way, everything is alive.

As energy is omnipresent, this would mean the intellect is also omnipresent, even though we are not aware of it. Just as every person who reads this, in all the random locations you are reading this in, can imagine the impact the smiling woman had upon me, you can witness the truth to the ability for information, and the output of my intellect, to be in multiple places at once. Yours, too, is also everywhere at once. The lesson learned from a blessing or mistake has always existed and will always exist, waiting to be rediscovered. The thoughts and feelings I had because of that woman's smile or because the puppy saved me from a snake, they have always existed and will continue to exist, everywhere at once, awaiting to be discovered. Right now, the feelings exist in the distant black hole and within the particle of oxygen you just breathed.

DNA transmission as a source of innate knowledge, could be a definite mode for our intellect to gain the fundamental knowledge we need. The data points and the mathematics which govern their function and application, all developed in an environment of increasing order. DNA itself is a product of intelligence as is its function. The more we learn, individually and collectively as a species, the more we can enhance the evolution of our DNA, enhancing our evolution, and enhancing future generations of people (our children). We continue to bring more order through education.

Education mustn't be formal institutions of learning, but education is the product of seeking knowledge and further developing the intellect. Education is the art and science of tapping into this omniscient, omnipresent energy, this intellect, and discovering its secrets, mysteries, and wisdoms. This process of seeking brings us more in tune of this infinite intellect and allows us to fight the forces of entropy. I may have just burned a candle, but it is guaranteed without my direct observation, the energies of the smoke, heat, and smell will end up somewhere as an intellectual property that will further enhance reality. From the old comes something better.

To us, information and the development of the intellect is progressive.

This means there is a constant progress towards higher levels, more refined levels. Like a child going from elementary school to middle school, so too is the progression of all mankind's knowledge. When someone like a Kukulkan or Baha'u'llah comes with new knowledge, they often testify their knowledge did not come from them, but that are in tune with the origins of all knowledge. Each time our knowledge progresses, our societies progress, and we understand scientific and spiritual lessons people from 5,000 years ago were unable to understand yet. Because we are bound by time due to our physical properties, our progression must go step by step. We do not have the capability for our neurons to be completely immersed into the infinite energies of the universe, but day by day, year by year, and era by era, we continue to evolve our knowledge. One year we observe fire, another we create fire, and in another we can create an instant inferno in an entire city with atomic power. This progression has come to us via these special people, who has taught us the principles of the golden rule, the golden rules of economy from Chapter 2, plus all the arts and sciences we experience today and into the future.

The process of learning will never end until maybe our neural networks, individually or collectively, are able to directly tap into that endless, all-encompassing energy. If energy is God, then the intellect must be God's Word. As long as we meditate, pray, think, and act, we can continue unlocking this intellect and make it our own. The intellect is the sole reason why energy can transform itself and transform matter. The intellect is the very essence of the beginnings and ends, the firsts and lasts, and from olds into news.

Knowing how our physical realities must be progressive as well as relative due to varying perspectives and the fact it interacts with an infinite energy and intellect, we can use this knowledge to further refine our modes of ordering ourselves. Economy, governance, corporations, non-profit organizations, and families can continue to be evolved and refined with increasing capacities from the intellect. Why do we rely on demand-side economics and myriads of currencies when these are old ways of doing things whose costs now outweigh their benefits? We can progress and develop more closely towards the seven golden rules of economy by taking the knowledge we have today and using our collective intellect to create better ways of doing business. Science and religion, if you look at both, agree outdated modes of doing things, for example old traditions, cannot serve us as education increases.

In the next chapters, I want to take the lessons of this chapter and apply them to genuine economic principles associated with intellectual property and an Ency based environment.

Chapter 11
ECONOMICS: THE INTELLECT AND PRICES

With the intellect being the primary component of energy transformation, it would make sense to look into the intellect's ability in shaping how markets work, currently and in an Ency economy. The intellect has been the foundation of human economy since our prehistory. It is the intellect which taught us fire, the first major breakthrough in energy transformation outside of hunting and gathering food. It continues today through all modes of living, from agriculture to high tech fields plus all the arts and sciences in between.

In most economic models, there is a point where the cost curves of supply and demand meet. This is known as the equilibrium price level. The equilibrium price level is determined to be the best price that markets for a given item will work best, that is when the needs of suppliers and consumers are met at the most optimal levels for both. In a large economy, no one ever truly knows what this equilibrium price level is and the equilibrium price is more of a theoretical construct to help with modeling. In reality, prices operate more like particles due in quantum mechanics. I say this because as soon as a person observes a phenomena, the phenomena has already changed, it has already moved. The very act of observing the phenomena initiates this movement. It is like trying to find a fighter jet in the sky with your eyes. You observe the sound but by the time you look to that sound, the fighter jet has already moved beyond your scope of focus. Prices are like this fighter jet, our speed of observation can never keep up with the speed of price change.

To further demonstrate this, you can create a demo account with any Forex trading platform. In these platforms, you can witness the constant changes in the price levels of the major currencies. You can also observe the changes over various periods of history, down to the minute. At any given point in time there are large swings, fluctuations, and a general motion similar to that of a wave. This wave is much like any electromagnetic wave except the wave sizes fluctuate. As soon as you observe a price, the prices has already changed. As soon as you observe a potential pattern, a phenomena changes the future course of events. Any news event or surprise can cause a new ripple or shock to the wave. This wave action demonstrates all of the experts of the world and the computer simulations used to trade have no idea what the price level of money is at any point in time. Due to this, with the price of money always in flux and always unknown to a degree, the price of everything purchased with money is also always in flux.

Why is it so difficult for prices to be truly known? The core of the difficulty is due to intelligence itself. Adam Smith first described prices in markets being established by rational agents who do their best to make decisions with the information available to them. The main criticism of this idea is each person has different pieces of information and not all of it is known in equal measure to all parties. Another way to say this is each person's own intellect is unique in its capacities and experiences. These unique factors cause people to value things differently and these values can fluctuate depending on circumstances. I know when I go into a store and I am hungry, a whole lot of food seems more valuable than if I went into the store on a full stomach. Immediate utility is important to us, how the item makes us feel both in the short-term and long-term, and whether or not the item will continue to be valuable over time are often times considerations we have when making purchases. Sellers also try to determine how their customers will evaluate these factors and also entice us by playing on our thoughts and feelings. Sellers with a great deal of information can establish effective prices which are above their costs and within an acceptable threshold many people are willing to pay.

Demand, when it is considered as the leading factor in economic activity, is really a study on human behavior and how our thoughts and feelings materialize into wants and needs. How will we obtain what we want and need? How much are we willing to give to obtain this? Is my new want and new need more important than other wants and needs? This study on human behavior, due to the nature of the intellect, is an infinite variable calculation which occurs at the speed of light but operating in a world which is much slower. Economists are able to determine key variables which bring about a high correlation, but they are poor indicators of future demand, or future needs and wants. They are good studies on if everything else remains the same, here is the trend, and here is the market. As soon as an indication of the future is found, it is no longer reliable. If so, there would be no market bubbles, recessions, constant fluctuations in the prices of money and commodities, and no panics by those we call experts.

Price discovery is the process actors in the economy enact when trying to determine the price of an item. In informal settings, this can be done through bartering and negotiation. In more formal settings this can be done as a shopper searches various retail outlets or online stores to determine price levels. Those supplying also use these processes to determine what someone is willing to pay. Price discovery is probably the most important component in the functioning of a smooth and free economic system.

The discovery of prices can happen on varying levels as well. Sometimes prices are based entirely on local factors, such as the price of an apartment in Manhattan or Lambasa as compared to a rural area. Prices can be determined regionally and even worldwide, such as with the petroleum markets. No matter the geographical determinant, prices often fluctuate. An interesting component of modern economics is associated with some of the consequences listed in Chapter 1, mostly from having the idea there can be infinite growth from finite resources. Demand side economics would normally favor deflation, which is the constant pressure to lower prices. We see this in how our markets are set up, where an entire industry can shift to another country where the factors of production cost less. However, supply side economics favors inflationary pressures, where prices rise. Currently, the world's monetary policies are set up to favor inflation thus favoring suppliers. Doing so helps reduce some of the uncertainties suppliers face but also limits the bartering power of those in demand.

As long as markets are currently established to favor supply, instead of treating both supply and demand equally, prices will always be in conflict. Having the Ency being the foundation of a new economic system will help reduce some of the uncertainties of pricing. The first and immediate effect is the price of money will relatively be constant, as there is only one currency in the market. The next effects will come from knowing the Ency is based upon units of energy, such as the kilowatt hour. A central bank cannot create Ency from nothing and can only be created as new energy is created within the economy, such as from agriculture, energy capture, and energy transformation. The only uncertain factors which will remain are the true wants and needs of people, instead of the imaginary passions and wants.

This chapter is mostly a simple synopsis of considering the intellect in establishing prices. There are other factors which favor the supply side when associated to the intellect and these factors also inhibit the ability to reach equilibrium pricing. Tariffs, quotas, sales/VAT/excise taxes, and the unequal application of these methods greatly influence markets. Also, the creation of monopolies, especially in regards to intellectual properties, greatly reduces the negotiating power those in demand have. The next couple of chapters will look into intellectual property, how it is currently managed in economy, how it could be managed in the Ency economy. Also, I want to provide a real life example of real estate markets in evaluating the effects of how we use our intellect. □

Chapter 12
LAW: WHAT IS INTELLECTUAL PROPERTY?

This will be a very short chapter designed to bring about how intellectual property came into being through the legal systems, their pros and cons, as well as their contributions to society. Intellectual property takes the form of copyrights, patents, trademarks, and even trade secrets.

In the United States, intellectual property in the form of copyrights have existed since the country first formed. Patents became protected in 1840 although inventions were protected outside of patent law. Copyrights were actually first introduced in 16th century Europe as a means to limit free speech. For an idea to become published, the right to copy had to be legally granted. If the idea was against the government's wishes, the idea would not be published. The original intention of a copyright was thus to restrict publishing of ideas unless the right was granted. Today in the USA, the right to copy is handled by the private sector. In theory, this will prevent the government from restricting ideas being published, although it is also well known many publishers of copyright do practice censorship. Sometimes the line between government censorship and private sector censorship cannot be easily discernible. Here is the example of Joseph Smith in 1843 and 1844, living in Nauvoo, Illinois. He was the founder of the Church of Jesus Christ of Latter Day Saints, a mayor, a judge, a general, and the owner of several businesses. One of these businesses was a printing press for one of newspapers. The newspaper would not publish any idea which was critical of Smith or any organization he was heavily involved with, such as the LDS church. Was this government or private censorship? Today there are many individuals outside of government with the resources and ability to influence which ideas reach government, and this feedback also works in reverse. In theory then, a copyright is at first a mode to regulate the publication of ideas by those who have the right to copy.

Copyrights are also a great form of creating wealth. When a copyright is granted, depending on the country you live in, the author and publisher have exclusive rights to the distribution and profit from the published work. If the published idea is popular and well managed, both author and publisher have a high profit potential. This creates an incentive to seek a copyright. Now, all ideas may not be original, but the presentation and methodology of the idea is protected. Not every item copyrighted brings financial success but it does ensure if there is profit, the profit remains with its creator. What if the idea is popular but the distribution has been limited? This type of model has regularly been used as a form of censorship. Another way is to price a copyright much higher than the market price. These types of actions by a publisher ensures they retain exclusive rights to publish and distribute, but any ideas the publisher does not want in the public can be withheld.

The enforcement of copyright law is quite difficult. Once the book, magazine, newspaper, or other publication is made public, the print is now available. One book could be shared by a hundred people, such as in a library. One magazine article can be translated in 100 languages which the copyright may not have protected against. Once an idea is manifested, it is virtually uncontrollable. I write this book believing in this fact, yet I find value in writing this.

Patents eventually developed to reward innovations and inventions. A patent grants a monopoly to the creator for a limited time and for only what is listed in the patent. In the USA, a patent can exist for 20 years or longer, depending on if it is extended. I personally find interesting the promotion of issuing a monopoly on the patent. The USA was created under the idea of having a free-market economy conducive to capitalism, yet at the individual level monopolies are promoted and encouraged. This practice itself, having two principles in conflict with each other, cause conflict in the rest of the country. What is the total effect on the USA economy? We can take a look at the GDP per capita of the United States before 1840 and after. Once patent law was refined, the economic growth per capita remained constant. Only after 1935 did the GDP per capita grow at a higher rate. Something else must have happened in 1935, or near 1935, to bring much larger growth. Patents were not the driver of growth.

What happens during a monopoly? In a monopoly, a business is able to charge a price higher than with competition. In competition, there would still be theoretical profits to be made, but the total pie would be shared with multiple companies. Also, a monopoly, due to the higher prices, ensures there is a sense of scarcity for the product being sold. Scarcity means only a certain number of people can purchase the item and receive some type of benefit from its use. Often times then, the poor are priced out from the monopoly. What if the monopoly is created in a good or service required for survival or for a needed cultural construct? This happens in the pharmaceutical industry for example, where research and development for drugs is extremely expensive. The development of many drugs would not exist without the monopoly incentive. This also leaves the costs beyond the reach of the poor, or to be shared through taxation or social insurance.

I also believe in many ways, the decisions we make seem to favor the reduction of competition by creating oligarchies or monopolies. Any company which can become the best at what it does for the right price will be chosen by a majority of consumers, at the cost of other market participants. Often times this cost is fatal to the businesses. Often times a company such as Wal-Mart may enter a local market and within a short-period, create a local retail monopoly. Small locally owned retailers were "driven out" not by Wal-Mart, but by the majority of consumers choosing a superior business model. We lament the few choices in cable or internet providers, yet, consumer choices created this phenomena. If the free-market then, favors short-term monopolies, are they inherently bad? If they are bad, then do consumers make bad decisions against their own social welfare?

The crux to these answers can be answered with the final question. What is property? So far with intellectual property I have described briefly two types of legally protected intellectual property, in a prior chapter discussed the intellect, but never have I discussed property. What is property? This answer, if you look at external sources, is not an easily agreed upon concept. Property can be something physical or intangible, it defines the ownership to a specified entity, an ownership which grants rights no one else may exercise, an ability to sell or trade, as well as exclusivity. Exclusivity itself is a monopolizing effect.

Let us start with the basic idea of land rights. Land rights have been defined as a right of the individual, the right of a state, or the right of the commons. In the USA today, land rights are usually that of the individual or state. Individual land rights allows a person to own a specific area of land as defined in a government issued title. The government may have certain regulations limiting the use of the specific land, but the title grants exclusive rights to those actions to the individual. The individual thus may use the land for recreation, profit, or remain idle for a future purpose. The right to the land is only revoked upon sale to another, or in special circumstances, the seizure of the property according to a legal precedent. The right to own land, in a way, made land valuable through both scarcity and profit from its inherent means of production. Prior to the USA being formed into its current boundaries, indigenous nations usually did not recognize individual property rights, only the rights of state or the commons.

Adam Smith in the Wealth of Nations describes how land rights can create both extreme wealth and poverty, both of which become government sanctioned. He did not observe a path to moderation in this kind of system. Earlier in the book, I described if there is an inherent right to land, then all should have access to exercise this right. Often times land rights have been used to create scarcity or to deprive others access which had prior existed. When an American, for example, exercised their right to claim a piece of land as theirs, they subsequently denied the right of, for example, the Cherokee Nation, to keep what was theirs. Because the Cherokee did not have a legal system recognizing individual property rights, the first person to exercise this right thus earned the right. Immediately, wealth was transferred through force, causing a consolidation of wealth to few and poverty to a larger population. This means individual land rights, at the origins of the United States, was granted only to a certain population on a first-come basis. Eventually this has expanded to allow all USA people the right to own land, but by this point in time, most available and productive land was already owned. Expanding the rights to all people drove up scarcity, consolidating wealth even further to fewer people.

Property rights then, were not necessarily about this innate human right to own property. Property rights were about the innate desire by people to reduce competition to obtain rights at a low cost and to protect those rights to drive up the cost. This of course is only sustainable by obtaining new property for free, which is usually associated with an act of war. If this is how property was originally managed in the USA, then what was the purpose in establishing intellectual property?

Intellectual property exists because people want to profit from an idea before another does. It is our nature to desire a monopoly as a seller, but to promote competition as a buyer. If anything of value can be controlled and restricted, then a profit can be consolidated to one while depriving others. However, can things of the intellect be completely controlled or restricted? Thomas Jefferson, who was on the board of the first patent office in 1790 believed it could not be, but still promoted the idea a person should profit for their intellect.

I personally believe in the golden rule of economy regarding moderation. Human nature tends towards both inflation as a seller and deflation as a buyer, and as a monopoly for the former and competition for the latter. If there is to be any system which can both provide for individual profit and provide for optimal social good, there must be moderation built into the system. Monopolies should not be completely eliminated, but they should not exist for an excess of time. Individual property rights should be enabled in such a way individuals are not neglected. In the end, the intellect will automatically cause progression on the individual and collective level. The discoverer of any knowledge, even though this knowledge has always existed, should be rewarded for introducing this knowledge. Likewise, this knowledge should not be restricted to the point only a few have access. Also, in the USA and many other countries, an inventor must pay to have a recognized patent. This favors the wealthy as they have the resources to file versus a poor person already struggling. If intellectual property is a right for all, then once again, all should have access to this right.

My last thought is the world has hundreds of different legal systems which manage intellectual property. Many times an individual must register their patent with multiple governments to comply in multiple markets. In a globalized economy, the legal system should be consolidated to where all are at least abiding by the same rules. This would require worldwide consultation about intellectual property, but a consultation not only dominated by the wealthy who would profit the most from certain rules.

In the next chapter I will now revisit the case of the MP3 and imagine how intellectual property can exist in a just manner in an Ency economy.

Chapter 13
ECONOMICS: ENERGY TRANSFORMATION & EDUCATION

The purpose of the intellect within the economy is to transform energy into something more valuable. The end product of these transformations will either create tangible products and services or intangible ones. What is the value of each kind in an Ency economy?

First, I will revisit the MP3 scenario. Music has always been a product which is difficult to price and difficult to manage. I remember when I was a kid, my sisters and I would often take blank cassette tapes and record our favorite songs from the radio. Sure, the quality was not great but it served the purpose. We could, for a cost much less than we could buy the single or album, listen to songs we liked. This was easy for us, but was probably not an outcome the record companies worked towards. The record companies have spent considerable resources in refining their product so that it is more difficult for consumers to listen to their products for free. This has become more challenging as technology advances. For a while there was Napster allowing music file-sharing, but legal action ended this enterprise. Then there was the Pirate Bay and torrents allowing music file-sharing, but many governments have worked together to end these types of services. Still today, there are streaming sites and the ability of friends and family to copy music files directly from each other.

When Apple created a new standard for selling and pricing songs and albums on their iTunes marketplace, they worked in conjunction with the record companies to establish security and pricing. They did not work with the buyers of music, you and me. The goals for each party were simple. Consumers were seeking music through the internet and there were no legal methods to do so where record companies could make a profit. Apple was wanting a platform to make increased demand for their iPods and new iPhones, where their devices would drive the demand for a new music marketplace and the marketplace could drive demand for their devices. Eventually an agreement came to fruition where music would have digital rights management to protect the intellectual property and the music would be priced equally among three different price tiers. The record companies would get a cut of the profits, Apple would profit, and consumers had a legal way to purchase digital music.

The iTunes service became hugely popular and even today, is one of the leading marketplaces for music. Digital rights management has become less important in the iTunes business model, but this has not seemed to hurt the demand for legal sources of digital music. Record companies also seem to be doing well, with more and more independent labels entering the market while the largest companies continue to create increasing amounts of music. This was all done while establishing an extremely simple pricing model for all digital music in the marketplace, a pricing model replicated by other marketplaces such as Amazon.

Businesses and consumers have always had a difficult time in establishing prices for the creative arts. The MP3, a book, software, images, and video have always suffered from the problem of never being scarce. Each can be easily replicated and shared. A book can be shared for free through a library or loaned through a friend. Software can be installed onto multiple devices, although for-profit software companies are figuring out more clever ways to manage this problem. A trend I've been noticing in all of the artistic fields is simplistic pricing. In a shared marketplace, all products are priced in certain tiers. All major video games releases tend to be $60 as of today for one example. Independent sellers still have varying prices, but I imagine they have a harder time selling their products.

The simple thing is this, a price is the only way to measure the total value an intellectual property has for an individual. The creator understands their costs in terms of time, materials, and competitors. A consumer understands only the utility or happiness an intellectual property provides. A unique intellectual property can be priced quite highly in the hopes this single work will provide a great amount of happiness for one individual. Paintings and sculptures are great examples of this. However, a print of the painting will be sold at a much lower price. The artist understands the print is not quite the same quality as the painting, but the artist can now provide those with some happiness a sellable product.

What I find intriguing is how some intellectual properties can eventually become worth millions of dollars. This is possible with our current economic system where infinite growth is designed into the system, despite finite resources. One painting by a Renaissance-era artist can be worth 500,000 meals, just to put some random number to this example. A painting in an art fair could be worth about 500 meals. A part of me feels it is wonderful how wealth can be created through the creation of intellectual property, while another part of me is concerned when our valuation of certain creations cause us to value other things less, such as the livelihood of the farmer who feeds us.

With the Ency, the only way the money supply can grow is if our collective energy supply also grows. The intellect, no matter how we use it and develop it, requires the connection to outside sources of energy within our physical plane of existence. To say it more simply, our economy can only grow the better we use outside sources of energy. Thankfully, we are blessed with the sun which provides more energy than we have learned how to use. This solar energy is the only outside source we can tap into to keep adding more energy to our civilization and economy. The more energy the world can capture and transform, the better organized we can be and the more wealth we can also have. When this happens, the more Ency which can enter the money supply. If we are inefficient in energy, such as introducing temporary energy sources such as petroleum, there could be fluctuations in the amount of Ency in the system.

If you combine an ever growing population, a scalable energy based currency, and an economy whose foundation is agriculture and a guaranteed right to a means to produce Ency, we will have the world's first economic system which can reduce or eliminate poverty while still encouraging growth. How can we ensure the world has the ability to regularly and consistently transform outside energy to ensure regular and consistent growth? The answer is through education.

Education, outside of solar energy, would be the primary means to capturing outside energy by tapping into the universal intellect for human use. Education is the means towards knowledge, creativity, and developing the sciences to better all of mankind. Today, I would say much of our education is quite poor throughout the whole world. I say this because the focus of education is not often the search for knowledge for the sake of knowledge, but education has become about indoctrinating a population to merely become productive workers. Each year, a smaller percentage of the world's population, despite the world becoming increasingly literate, are able to create. The ability to create or manage creation is the foundation for entrepreneurship.

Let's look at the pharmaceutical industry for a brief snapshot of our current dilemma. As of this writing, there are about 360 companies who create drugs for legal consumption. A great many of these companies provide only off-brand medicines and thus aren't necessarily creators, but copiers at a reduced cost. If we take a world population of about 7 billion people, we can say only 1 out of 19 million people currently own or are the CEO of a pharmaceutical company. It is also safe to say a majority of the world's population seek some type of benefit from this industry such as to prolong life or sustain a high quality of life. It is also safe to say a majority of people seek an education. Why is it only 1 out of 19 million people are able to be educated well enough to start, create, or manage a pharmaceutical company?

A part of the answer is the costs associated with research and development. In the USA for example, the development process from start to finish, if the new drug is approved, can average about 6 years. This would be 6 years of paying researchers, conducting expensive experiments, maintaining laboratories, complying with regulations, and other associated costs. This entire process exists for a drug which may not bring a profit for the company. Some studies have estimated the average cost for this entire cycle could be between $800 million and $1.4 billion. This process isn't conducive to sole proprietorship or even small business. A business has to be well capitalized in this system. The only other alternatives right now are universities and government research.

One reason why this process has such high costs is the inefficiencies of competition but also the cost of this education. To earn a Master's degree in pharmacology, a two year program can cost anywhere from $30,000 to $40,000. This cost makes the education program accessible by only a small portion of the world's population. On top of this, this person may not become educated in business management. This part is import. For example, the CEO of Pfizer started his career with Pfizer as an auditor and never worked in research. The value for a pharmaceutical company is not only solely in pharmaceutical sciences, but how a business person can leverage the capital to bring together the necessary resources to create a new drug. This has to come in the face of competition. One of the other companies may be researching the same type of medicine. Who succeeds at doing so first enters the market first, establishing necessary market position. If the process required hundreds of millions of dollars, the latter company may not be able to profit from its research.

I believe in order to make the transformative power of education to work within an Ency dominated economy, there should be differentiation between seeking education for the sake of knowledge and seeking knowledge for the sake of profit. I personally am happy when both can exist together but after experiencing the university system of today, I believe about 90% of all students are not interested in seeking knowledge but do so solely for the opportunity of profit. However, seeking knowledge for the sake of knowledge is the foundation of all innovation. The only pathway to start transforming the educational system to be knowledge oriented is to promote the pathways of creation. The subjects emphasized would combine the sciences with the arts, moderated by regular teaching of values and ethics. Let students ask their own questions about what they observe in the world, and teachers train them how to seek these answers using math, literature, science and how to express these answers through the arts. Knowledge is most useful, as any capitalist knows, when knowledge has an outward expression.

Competition also needs to be moderated by cooperation. At all phases of the educational system, competition is often enforced over the benefits of cooperation. Consultation and cooperation can further transform the power of education by allowing the belief to share in knowledge, wisdom, and methodologies. Eventually, in the long-view of things, intellectual properties as being a right to the individual will fade to being the right of many, perhaps all. What if there were 5,000 pharmaceutical start-ups working towards collective goals the common public deems necessary or vital to their well-being? Whoever first discovers a key source of knowledge of a methodology is given a one-time reward while at the same time, this knowledge is shared with the rest to start the next stage of discovery? Both the individual's reward for innovation through competition is maintained, but not at the sacrifice of cooperation. Remember, the products of the intellect can be restricted and slowed down, but it is inevitable these products will eventually be accessible to all.

In such scenarios, we can determine the value of this energy. The researchers can seek their price and negotiate with the public. These can happen instantaneously with current technology. Once we have an economy based on the Ency, our calculus will change. How much value did this energy transformation give to the family, village, city, state, or world?

A true education is vital to the continued sustainable development of a just economy. To ensure justice and reduce poverty, cooperation is vital and needs to be built into all systems. Primary schools, trade schools, universities, and on-the-job training need to value cooperation and ethics at all levels, to ensure education is both for the individual good and the good of all of us. Education allows for the development of the intellect, an intellect which is provided to us from this omnipresent and omnipotent source which has ordered our world from seeming chaos into something organized. This intellect, which may not be capable of being owned by an individual for any length of time, is the source of all energy transformation and thus, the source of economic growth in an Ency economy.

Chapter 14
FAMILY: EDUCATION & DEVELOPMENT

In the last chapter, I introduced a concept of developing pharmaceutical research needs through the public. However, as many people are usually skeptical of, government led research sometimes ends up being led by politics, election-oriented concepts, and other motives led more by power and corruption than for the public interest. Sometimes the needs of government and its people do intersect, such as research programs for HIV research or protecting the most precious of habitats from human development. In fact, if protected areas are an indication of the priorities of mankind, it should be noted about 10-15% of the world's land area is protected, leaving 85-90% open for development. This would lead us to assume about 90% of a government's decisions focus on concepts and policies for infinite growth in the current economic systems, where only 10% of resources are suitable for a long-term view of the future. Given how government needs, public needs, and individual needs intersect, we should look into ways where this intersection can better fulfill the needs of this generation, the future generations, and allow for an increasing quality of life for all.

I believe once again this all starts with the family and the collection of a community's families. The key value to explore in this chapter is equality. What does equality mean? To me, the totality of one's self is not more nor less than the totality of another's self. The sum of all parts of me is equal to the sum of all parts of you. Does this mean each person has the exact same capacities and potentials? Not at all. Depending on who we are, we feel things differently, we think differently, and express ourselves differently. How we interact with the ever-present energy is unique to each of us. Most social scientists would agree to the equality of all people in regards to race, ethnicity, nationality, gender, and any other identifiable attribute a person cannot control at birth.

Equality in the family and its expression often has had many controversies, especially when looked at among varying cultures throughout the world. The easiest way to measure equality is if the individual adult members of the family are free to live their lives as they choose, for their own individual benefit and the benefit of the rest of the family. Today there are many factors which inhibit this equality. Some are well known and others are never discussed. Usually the focus is on women's rights, but it doesn't have to be exclusive of women. The key to identifying any equality is measuring how effective a person is able to live their life as he or she chooses.

What if a mother or a father wants to educate their child at home? For this imagination I won't bring up the age of the child. This child could be newborn or even an adolescent. How easy is it for one of the parents to make this decision? In some communities, this is a difficult decision. Can one parent earn enough working a full-time job to provide food, clothing, and shelter for three people? In many places this is not possible, especially with the current economic system. If this is not possible, how free is the other parent in their decision? In this case there may not be a choice. To me, lacking a choice due to the system we live in is an oppressive system.

There are many other types of decisions which can be affected by various sources of oppression. Who can one marry? Can one open a business in their community? Can one walk down a street safely? How may one dress? Can I receive an education? These types of questions are endless. The answers depends mostly on how your family and community are organized and are heavily influenced by the types of education received. Sources of education can come from a parent, extended family number, religious organization, daycare, public and private schools, books, libraries, museums, and the environment itself.

To ensure an education of equality, each of these institutions must also value and teach equality. Right now equality is sometimes taught at a superficial level, but not as a core value underlying all other teaching. In the USA, one way I see equality being taught superficially would be during the "Black History month" encouraged by the federal and state governments. This is a month to encourage a greater number of educational efforts to understand the history and accomplishments of Americans of African origin. A key highlight for many is the celebration of Dr. Martin Luther King, Jr. However, the reason why a special month is created is because often times, the contributions of black Americans are not recognized in the normal educational process. Having a black history month as a favor and "special" time demonstrates the inequality of the normal educational process, the inequality inherent in the system. Also, many times the history of black Americans is often reduced down to Dr. Martin Luther King, Jr. and a few other people. Neglected in the history is how black Americans originated in America and the full consequences of history, further eroding the true foundation of equality. Another area highly affecting equality as a teaching are within the religious institutions. Many teach there was one creator who created everyone, yet these same institutions teach people of their particular faith are more deserving of salvation than others. This superiority leads to inequality through obvious ways such as the deprivation of equal human rights, to more subtle experiences as saying others need saved or a parent's disapproval of an interfaith relationship.

With the need for equality to be a core foundation of the entire educational process, we need to make sure all has equal access to education. Many times those in poverty are required to partake in an ineffective education process when compared to those who are not in poverty. Throughout the world, poor children suffer from large class sizes, lack of access to technology or new books, and the life of living in a system where few will ever be able to leave the grasp of poverty. Many children end up not valuing education as it doesn't take care of their immediate needs of survival, needs they often need to help their families with. Education alone won't directly eliminate poverty, but it would be the foundation to ensure no one finds it acceptable to have poverty. This will cause a paradigm shift, where more and more will work together to eliminate poverty.

The other benefit of having equality as the foundation of education will be the development of unity. Feeling each is equal, despite various capacities in arts, science, personality, and such will allow the nurturing of a people who may have more compassion and empathy. This will lead to higher degrees of cooperation and consultation instead of conflict and competition. This won't be an instantaneous process but will be gradual, its effects growing with each new generation.

Will families encourage equality? I genuinely hope so. Many economists have demonstrated the cost of inequality in the economic system. The entire world's economic potential could currently be about only 30% utilized due to the inefficiencies inequality bring. Will families care about the well-being of other families equally to theirs? This question isn't about each family earning the same. I do not promote equal pay for everyone. Instead, this question is about whether or not people will care about each person or family achieving a minimum income to meet their needs and having the access and opportunity to work towards this income. Will families encourage an education which finds poverty unacceptable? Will families encourage teaching cooperation with neighbors, near and far? Will families work together to encourage individuals to have both freedom of choice and action, while also promoting the benefit of others?

Combining a focus of education and a sustainable and social economic development will fit perfectly within the Ency economy. By ensuring each family within the world is utilizing the same currency, the same calculus, and encouraging the production and transformation of energy by any person in the world who wants to earn a living, we will have a system which can be sustained for many generations to come. I believe this education, being found on the foundation of equality, will bring us closer to the economic Golden Rules. I believe usury would be strongly discouraged, if not eliminated, as it makes neighboring families weaker. We are only as strong as our weakest link, much like a chain. I also believe moderation would be encouraged, or at least an average of all parts without a great deviation therefrom. Combined with the other natural aspects of using the Ency, justice in our economy can be achievable. Education will drive the transformation of energy, to provide the world with more Ency as well as making new innovations which can be of profit to individuals and to neighbors.

Chapter 15
FAITH & SCIENCE: LOVE

This chapter will take an alternative view as to what love is. The love series of chapters will be quite short compared to the others, as there will only be a couple broad economic principles involved. This isn't to say they aren't any more important, and in fact, this may be the most important part of the book. However, I hope to keep the ideas as broad as possible as hopefully I have been throughout the preceding chapters. One of my goals is to allow the power of interpretation and expression to be manifested in the varying ways they do. There is a great power in embracing diversity while acknowledging oneness. Much like the guidance of nutritionists when they express the importance of a colorful diet, or the need for many types and colors of flowers to make a most beautiful garden, diversity is what brings all the individual and special attributes together into a complete whole.

Despite the diversities of all aspects of creation to include the expressions of our limitless and eternal energy, we can see certain patterns form from this greater intellect. Mathematics has been a great tool to understanding and discovering these patterns, or for providing concrete proofs of things we observe and hypothesize. It is rather remarkable how consistent the modes of energy are in the organization of the world. A simple observation from ancient societies is the use of the numeral pi within all circles and spheres. Knowing how pi exists as a common coefficient has led to many equations describing the area and volume of these shapes and also the use of energies by objects on circular paths. Pi is not a random occurrence but a conscientious symbol existing within all layers of creation, affecting both the realms of matter and that of energy. Pi has also guaranteed there is never an object completely alone because every object creates just enough transformation of time and space (energy) which causes other objects to be attracted to it.

When I was a child, my attention deficit disorder often led me down some pathways which led to some interesting observations. Despite how often I would be told to not play with my food, I could not resist. The cereal Lucky Charms was, and still is, one of my favorites. Part of the allure as a child was of course the sugary sweetness and the colorful marshmallows. However, my play with them unlocked some intriguing mysteries. As I would separate the cereals by shape, color, or even their food type such as oat and marshmallow, I noticed I would have a hard time keeping one piece of cereal separate from the others. This became a challenge of sorts to see if I could keep one piece of cereal balanced within the 2% milk in such a way that it would not drift and come into contact with other pieces of cereal or the bowl itself. I discovered if I left this single piece of oat or marshmallow to its own devices, it would always drift towards another cereal. My first theory on the matter was the milk still has flow, much like the small lake I lived near. But, if I could keep the milk motionless for a long time while keeping the piece of cereal in place, the moment I let go the cereal would still drift away from the center. My next observation became important. I later noticed the milk seemed to fold underneath the cereal and fold under the bowl. Imagine the milk reaching the cereal bowl and it folds under towards the bottom of the bowl. There was never an "edge" to the milk and the milk seemed to bend on its own accord. This bending of the milk then is what would cause the cereal to drift. Once a piece would get close enough to another piece, both would speed up towards each other until they were in contact. The two pieces of cereal would combine together to make a slightly deeper bend in the milk. More cereal would start going towards these two pieces unless they were in contact with the bowl. The pieces in the middle would also eventually drift towards the edge until every single piece was somehow in contact with the bowl, directly or indirectly. My theory was the bending at the bowl's edge was more powerful than the bending of the smaller cereal.

I had not known it then but many years later, shortly outside of high school I learned I was observing a component of the theory of relativity. This was partially gravity (energy) but the bending of space. I learned it is easy to observe large objects, such as the sun, earth, and moon interact in these ways. Each object causes a bend in the invisible matter and energy. This bending causes matter and energy to be attracted to each other. Science has demonstrated, that much like my Lucky Charms, even small objects have this effect. The only reason why these objects do not collide is because they are moving at such great speeds, meaning there is so much energy being used in their orbit, they are able to resist this attraction to a degree of near neutrality.

When observing the shapes of orbits, we can always observe the coefficient of pi. To me, this is a proof of the intellect at work. No matter how far back astronomers observe into space, and thus observe into ages past, we learn pi is constant no matter the age. Pi then, is part of this eternal intellectual energy and a sign into the laws of attraction, if any were to be formally worded.

There are other forces of energy which cause attraction. We observe magnetism through electromagnetic energy. A positive force and a negative force attract each other. When we observe atoms, we observe the nucleus of the proton and neutrons being orbited by electrons, although not in the exact manner of the celestial bodies. An electron is more of a wave-particle and thus operates a little differently. No matter what though, no matter how far we zoom in or zoom out, we see varying mechanics where energy causes attraction. Each mechanic can be described fairly confidently with mathematical models due to their consistent nature.

A common scientist would not describe these forms of attraction as love, but I will. The eternal, omnipresent energy which creates with an intellect has created in such a way that love is everywhere. Love, or the infinite modes of attraction we are able to observe with reliable mathematical probability, is also eternal and omnipresent. It is a function of the intellect. If you are skeptical though, let's look at it another way.

We have been able to observe to varying degrees what happens when this natural order of attraction is forced to break, when objects and energies designed to be attracted to each other are forced to separate. For my Lucky Charms, my cereal mostly waited patiently until I allowed them to be free to be together, but what happens when an atom is split? For every atom, there is the process of nuclear fission. Depending on the size of the atom, its effects can be much different. Still, each releases a relatively high amount of energy for its size. By the time we get to the heaviest atoms, such as Uranium, you have a process which can cause much destruction relative to the atom's size. In this case, forcing this law of attraction to break is a relatively violent act. What would happen if any two objects, naturally bound together by their natural force, were to be separated? Usually those two objects will cease to exist as they are, or objects needing their union will cease to exist.

We also see when individual objects naturally come together, great things are created. The best example I can think of is during reproduction, or the fact that as I write this book, I am comprised of trillions of independently living cells which must be attracted to each other in order to function as the entity known as me. If even one of my cells is injured or killed from an outside source, I feel it and it affects me negatively. My cells love each other, much like the electron loves the proton, and the earth loves the sun. Each example exists because of its design.

What do the world's faiths say about this phenomena? The easiest example I can think of is in the Qur'an there are verses which say all of creation is created in pairs, and in creation are spheres upon spheres. Every faith I have learned about does place value in various forms of pairs. Some express a female and male duality of the creator, while others emphasize forms of justice such as reward and punishment. Many teach about good and evil, peace and war, and many forms of duality. Most teach these things with the idea of organizing the world in altruistic ways, where there can be a greater amount of attractive forces than the destructive ones.

One thing I learned in the observations of attraction in nature is each are endowed with a natural sense of moderation. Usually, these forms exist in such a way where there is attraction, but there is a balancing energy which keeps this attraction from being too strong. If the objects collide, they cease to exist in productive ways. Life could not exist if the law of attraction was not moderated. Earth could not exist if it could not keep the appropriate space from the Sun, and neither could we. When the attraction is too strong, then we have destruction. Sometimes other objects get in the way of the attraction, such as when Earth gets in the way of an asteroid, but when left to each's own energies, there is attraction but only enough to attract without destruction.

I feel religion has often been this way. As mankind, in its evolution and progression, has developed its collective intellect, we often find ways to either find modes of attraction which are too strong or find ways to sever the natural order of attraction. Both pathways tend to be destructive in their result. Whether it has been the faith of the Wanka Tanaka, Buddhism, or the Baha'i Faith (as 3 of many examples), love is a primary teaching. Love within religion often is focused on loving other people such as parents, neighbors, and even enemies. Our faiths teach to love our Creator as well as Creation itself. This creation includes the various living creatures, the environment, and many things known and unknown.

Certain types of love are often regulated by measures of moderation. Charity in some faiths is highly encouraged as an act of love, but one is never asked to give all they have to others. Sometimes there are set percentages as recommended, such as the well-known 10% tithe. Charity can be monetary or based on other methods of value, such as donated time. Other moderated forms of love occur within the sexual expression of love. This powerful expression is consistently moderated to either be within a monogamous relationship or a polygamous one with the consent of all.

Why are there religious moderations on love? Much like what has been expressed in the seven consequences of our current economy, we see many pathways of failure, conflict, and destruction when good things reach too far. Have you ever been in a relationship with someone you felt was obsessive, or have you been described as obsessive? Sometimes when a good thing goes too far in one direction, it causes pain. Too much charity can bring an individual hardship and too much sexual love can bring physical and psychological disease. Too much of any good thing creates dependence, limiting the true potentials of one's entire intellect. On the other side, too little of each also have the similar consequences.

When it comes to organizing the economy around a single world currency, we have to ensure the institutions in place and the methodologies used to measure success combine both the laws of attraction with the modes of moderation. Should there be a single worldwide central bank managed by bankers who own shares of private banks, or otherwise can profit from the central bank's policies? Should there be a team of scientists, not just financial or economic experts, who balance each other's expertise in such a way we can identify the measures of success?

For now, these measures of success must key on the production of energy, the transformation of energy, the production of the intellect, the transformation of the intellect, and various measures of our means of attraction. These means of attraction can take the form of measuring income inequality as we currently do, or find new ways to integrate qualitative measures of living. The UN has some effective measures using the Human Development Index. The final analysis, especially in regards to this chapter on love must always answer this question. How sustainable are we? How sustainable is my action? How sustainable is this quality of life?

Right now, as our world is currently organized, there are many who attempt a quality of life where, if those in poverty were able to achieve, would pressure the planet and our infrastructure in such a way a cataclysm would result. Utter chaos and destruction would be the result. This is not sustainable nor is it any expression of love for our children or our children's children. It is not an expression of love for the trees, the crops, the domestic animals, the wild animals, and everything in the air, ground, and water. Love, as it is an energy which will always exist, everywhere at all times, needs to be the primary calculation of our intellectual endeavors. Otherwise, all of our development goals, all the reforms and revolutions we people try to muster, will always fail.

In the next chapter, I will present the single biggest obstacle of love and how we can eliminate it in such a way we can empower our economies for a nearly unlimited growth.

Chapter 16
ECONOMICS: FENCES & UNITY

One day I was driving through the Great Plains of the United States. I enjoy road trips and sometimes when I do so alone, my mind has a chance to wander and reflect. Countryside driving is almost an act of meditation for me. During this particular drive, for some reason the fences stood out to me. No matter which road I took, whether it was a highway or some gravel road, no matter if I was still near some trees, green grassland, or some desert type shrubbery, there were fences. In fact, I do not recollect any space without fences. Sometimes I asked myself, what are the purposes of these fences? Who made the first fences here?

Some of the fences were being used to contain livestock. A sturdy fence or an electrical fence would surround herds of hundreds of cattle. Many of the fences did not appear to be containing anything, at least for the brief moments I would pass by. Maybe when they were not being used to contain livestock, maybe it was used to keep other animals and people out. I also realized the fence established a private claim to the land inside. The fence is the technological representative of the expression of a private right to land.

The fence is an old technology, first being documented in history associated with Greek conquests. The Greeks did not use fences in their homeland, but after a conquest, the foreign land would be divided up among interested parties. In this case, the fence represented conquest, domination, and private land ownership. This technology had spread throughout Europe, gaining particular popularity among the Romans. Both empires are ancient representatives of modern Western civilization and in a way represents the values of the West throughout the present day.

The fences I drove by in the Great Plains, despite their present day usage to contain livestock, are also representatives of conquest, domination, and private land ownership. Looking back into history, no less than 150 years ago the lands I was driving through had no fences. There may have been a stockade to provide communal protection, but not every piece of land was fenced. I imagine what the landscape would have looked like without fences. The wide open spaces of the Great Plains would seem even more vast, more open, and perhaps more great. I imagined I could see wild grasses and shrubs, with more frequent sightings of wildlife. Maybe I could see a large herd of bison slowing moving unimpeded. Maybe I could see a cougar chasing a pronghorn antelope. Maybe I could see one of the hundred different species of wild grouse which used to live there. That day I drove around, I mostly saw emptiness. This emptiness felt to me as a lack of movement, a lack of life, and an abundance of prior death. The Great Plains are not so great these days, although their outward beauty is still undeniable. The only containment fence I saw which had life were on the borders of Native American reservations. Those at a time were meant to symbolize the containment of an ethnic people although today we are convinced the fences are used to identify the private property outside the reservations. Fences then, are also a matter of cultural perspective and identity. A fence can be a sign of wealth and control to one while a fence can be a sign of poverty and loss of freedom.

Today, throughout the world, fences are now common in every context imaginable. Fences are used as decoration in many neighborhoods, to ensure privacy within a property, to contain criminals in a prison, to contain animals in a pasture, to separate national borders, and to separate ourselves. The fence is mostly associated with the idea of private property, ensuring the rights of an individual or the rights of a family. The fence separates individuals and separates families. Even the few communal places which remain, such as parks and places of worship, are often divided by fencing. Large cities may have parks fenced in so a certain population can't come in, such as the homeless. In today's political climate, we can also associate fences as an outward expression of keeping certain kinds of people safe from other kinds of people. Israel and Palestine is the most famous form of fenced boundaries, but they are becoming more common with each passing day.

These answers I came to as I drove around sometimes made me wonder and create even more questions. If a fence is used to keep a person from coming in, do we limit our own freedom by containing ourselves? Or do we hope we can control the gates so that we have all the control and choice and deny it to the others. Throughout this book, I've regularly made arguments about how the denial of freedoms can limit the potentials of economy. Despite the fence being associated with the organization and recognition of private property rights, fences are often used to deny free market forces.

Most economists will state an efficient economy is one where goods can quickly move from place to place. We often grant our goods more freedoms than we grant ourselves. Does my shirt made in Pakistan require a visa? Not at all. My shirt passed a customs inspection to ensure it wasn't opium or some other illegal good, and onward it went to my favorite store. An efficient economy depends on this low friction movement of goods. Government infrastructure is designed and planned around trading of goods. Roads, railways, ports, and their rules and regulations are all designed to move goods.

Another sign of an efficient economy is one where ideas can quickly move from place to place as presented earlier in the intellect section of this book. The final sign of an efficient economy is one where people can also move quickly move from place to place. Often times the movement of people happens at the same time as the movement of goods. However, this isn't as efficient as it seems. How easy is it for a person in a border city to move to the other side of the border for a job? This decision is quite difficult and must be planned well in advance. There is much bureaucratic friction limiting the speed upon which people can move.

I've seen fencing be used to purposefully limit the economic potentials of entire groups of people by restricting the movement of the people. Fence in a people and control the checkpoints and the group being controlled no longer can have an efficient free market. They become reliant upon those in control. This tactic has often been used for ethnic cleansing or a precursor to other types of genocide. Sometimes fencing isn't as obvious, such as railroad tracks in large cities. Cities often make the crossings of railways illegal except at designated road crossings. In cities where the poor often live on one side of a railway and the wealthier on the other, the railway establishes limited control upon the poor's ability to move and practice efficient economy, eroding their ability to move up the economic ladder. In days of segregation, this type of control was used to ensure the development of a majority while the minority was denied similar opportunities.

You see, the fence gets in the way of the greatest potentials an economy can achieve. Look at all the empty space I saw in the Great Plains. It will remain empty as no one can come and make use of the land. Look at the empty lots and abandoned buildings in cities, especially ones ravaged by a changing economy. You often see fences surrounding them, reminders that even these places are owned and controlled by a private individual. This individual prefers to keep their right to the property instead of advancing the needs of the society. Let's look at it this way. If the Greeks felt fencing was only needed after conquest in foreign lands, then they knew Greeks themselves would not benefit. The fence, being a mode of conquest and war, was a mode of destruction, not a mode of construction. In Athens, the people did not need fences because their culture demanded unity, a unity which made them more powerful than their neighbors.

Our legal systems have evolved around the social construct of fencing. Many philosophers and social scientists point out a fence serves a purpose of protecting the land from ourselves. If we do not express our long-term interest in a property, we will use the land unsustainably. If we express our long-term interest in a property, we use it in a way to ensure its long-term use and value. Land was a mode of transferring wealth within a family, such as from parent to child. I totally understand this. I actually agree Western civilization needed some technology and legal system to keep us from destroying our own means. I support land-owning as a method of creating a livelihood, especially one where one can capture energy for profit, such as with agriculture, electricity, or where one can transform energy through intellectual capital. However, our use of fences, whether visible or invisible, need to be adapted. No longer should fences be viewed as a method to domination and control as this use impedes sustainable economic development. Fences should only be used where necessary, such as securing food.

What does it mean to love one's neighbor? How can our usage of fencing demonstrate love for one's neighbor? These are types of questions we should be asking, no matter if our neighbor is in an adjacent private property, or even a bordering country. With the development of the Ency, being a single world currency, the people associated with the economy need to be free to move as the economy requires. True competition requires a person's free movement, not just the free movement of a person's production. Once a person is free to move, such as to seek the best business opportunity or the best wage, we can determine the full value and potential of this person. Why should a shirt made in Indonesia have more freedom of movement than a person born in Jakarta? This is nonsense. The truth is these rules which enforce fences, such as requiring months to process a visa or the denial of visas, are invisible fences, born from ideas of protectionism, "us versus them" ideology, and a lack of love for one's neighbor.

The energy which empowers us is free and it can be everywhere at all times. The intellect which we interact with to discover, express, and transform our world is also free, able to be everywhere at all times. The love, the natural force of attraction throughout all modes of nature, is free and has been ordering all of creation since mankind has been aware of time. Our economic systems need to be based on these principles. If they are not, then we as a people can never be free. A fence restricts us, it restricts our movements, creates oppression, creates hate, causes segregations instead of unity, and prevents a truly natural and divine economy from ever existing.

The Ency will, in this case, work as a unifying symbol for all people. If I want Chicken Biryani in Bangladesh, despite being in sovereign countries, we will be able to communicate in the same form of money. We will have an outward common bond, although such bonds should exist due to our shared humanity. Instead of fences dividing us and dividing our thoughts and feelings, we will share the same calculus. Our worth will be based on our capacities, what we produce, what we create, and not due to being confined within a nation's fences or even the local fences. The economy will be about love for your family, and the love for another's family. This is what Unueco Partio is about.

Chapter 17
FAITH & SCIENCE: EVOLUTION

This will be the final chapter discussing faith and science. So far I have focused on the foundations of energy, the intellect, and love to help us imagine the potentials of having a single world currency called the Ency. I admit much of this is radical, although I myself hope to be moderate. I also realize much of what I have proposed would not realistically be implemented immediately. Change requires time, patience, and practice. This brings me to the subject of evolution.

The subject of evolution has been a great source of contention for many of religious backgrounds. The basic idea of the theory of evolution is biological organisms are subject to modification over time, through the acts of reproduction and survival. Some believe everything was created perfectly and thus was never in need of any change. There are many types of arguments in between these two simple statements covering a wide variety of subjects. However, my intention is to look at evolution differently and maybe make the case about how we need to embrace evolution to some degree, if not completely.

Biologically, I would like to tell the short story about gonorrhea. It is a disease which has existed since antiquity and may have even been referenced in the Old Testament in Leviticus 15. Governments in Europe even created laws in the medieval ages to force treatment of gonorrhea. With the modern advent of antibiotics, gonorrhea has developed resistance to all antibiotics but two. Even these two are showing signs of becoming ineffective and the World Health Organization believes there is a potential for a new epidemic. This short story testifies to two primary modes of change. The first is that of the bacteria called gonorrhea. The second is that of the human.

The first mode of change occurred due to gonorrhea's will to survive and reproduce. When an old treatment no longer worked, it was because there would be some surviving gonorrhea which would eventually reproduce and spread. The bacteria has an incubation period of 10-30 days. This means every 30 days, a new generation of gonorrhea emerges. Every 30 days, the genetic material of this bacteria has the potential to be modified during reproduction so the bacteria can be better able to survive. Over the course of 70 years since antibiotics were first used for treatment, gonorrhea has reproduced and survived through approximately 840 generations. The 840th generation is stronger and better adapted than the generation 70 years ago.

The second mode of change occurred due to the person's will to survive and reproduce. Mankind does not have the luxury of being able to reproduce quickly like a bacteria, despite our best efforts sometimes. Over 70 years, the average person has been succeeded by 2-5 generations, depending on factors such as culture and chance. We have not had the opportunity to adapt our biology as quickly as gonorrhea. Due to this, we have had to rely on our intelligence to try to stay a step ahead. We have tried to develop medicine, some of which were products of the scientific method, some which were not, to kill gonorrhea. We have tried to develop laws and regulations to identify and limit the spread of gonorrhea. Even our religious institutions have encouraged some behaviors which would limit the ability for gonorrhea to be successful. These are modes of our intellectual ability to adapt when our biology is unable to as quickly as needed.

No matter your political or religious views, there is definite and identifiable evidence of the adaptable nature of our intelligence. The intelligence is brought forth through our biology but our biology doesn't prevent the intelligence of adapting more quickly than the biology. By the time gonorrhea reached its 840th generation, mankind's intelligence has had the ability to adapt 840 times, maybe even more if you consider its potential.

How has mankind's intelligence demonstrated its adaptability in religion? The easiest example I can determine is the progression of historical prophets through the Abrahamic religions, although this progression is also evidenced in Hindu and aboriginal faiths as well. However, I am most familiar with the Abrahamic religions. Let me start with Adam and Eve. As far as documented in the book of Genesis and other apocryphal books, Adam and Eve were given very simple instructions to obey. This simple instruction proved to be difficult for them. For each successive generation, the instructions became more complex. By the time of Moses, there were complex laws and regulations. When Jesus came the instructions were less straight-forward and in the increasingly complex form of the parable. What is true is Adam and Eve were never given the same instructions as Abraham, Moses, Jesus, or any in between or any after. Their capacity wasn't as well developed. Perhaps their intellect wasn't as well developed.

What we know today is Adam and Eve did not have the knowledge we have today. We have the knowledge they had, plus the knowledge of 5,000 to 6,000 years later. If it is 6,000 years, this is about 400 generations if each person reproduced at the age of 15 (the fastest I would consider). Adam and Eve had not learned about medical science, nuclear power, skyscrapers, traffic lights, air conditioning, democracy, communism, gonorrhea, Jesus, or any other significant religious figure. We have had 400 generations to develop our intellect and our biology. It is definitely true in many ways, mankind has better adapted to survive and continue reproducing successfully while continuously striving for improvement.

I believe whole-heartedly we must embrace continued change and adaptation, especially in our methods of using our intellect. So far various intellectual endeavors have lagged in their progress and change as compared to others. Mankind has searched for answers by investigating the reality of creation on every level. We look into subatomic particles, galaxies, the deep ocean, and our own consciousness. Each day brings us new knowledge, new developments, and new agents of progression and change. Why can't our modes of economy adapt as well?

The annals of human history have shown very few changes in how we approach economy. Supply and demand are the pillars of development and fulfillment of our wants and needs. Our modes of transaction have only used direct trading or an intermediary mode of exchange, such as modern currency. Modern currency itself has rarely changed in its form. There have always been multiple standards but all based on the idea of a physical commodity or a fiat. Little else has ever changed.

Bringing into use the Ency would be an entire paradigm shift. It would be the next step in the evolution of man's intellect with the purpose of survival and progress. The challenges with implementing an energy-based currency would be many, but the merits of such would bring about a better system. The primary changes needed would require a new institution to replace central banks. This institution would need to represent the individuals who use the currency, so thus the Ency would need to be a democratically represented currency. The institution would need experts in multiple fields to identify the energy cost and production for the full spectrum of human activity. This would require energy scientists, economists, psychologists, sociologists, educators, clergy, and others. The representation would need to come from every culture and nation and from each type of socioeconomic class.

These ideas about the Ency, this loose framework established in this book, can be a great starting point for those who embrace science and/or faith to achieve a positive change in our world economy. Energy and its transformation has definite applications for the economic benefit for all. This evolution requires an evolution to not only our mode of transaction, but our calculations in what we value, how we save, how we invest, how our businesses are run, and even how our businesses are structured.

One example I would consider would be the structure of corporations. Today, corporations are commonly considered legal entities made up of many individuals. These individuals include the board of directors, shareholders, and employees. Often times individuals who are responsible for the affairs of the corporation, such as the CEO, do not share full responsibility. For example, a corporation may be held liable for an illegal action, but the individuals responsible are not liable for the illegal action. The first progressions to the corporate structure would be to restore individual accountability. Only people can vote, only people can speak, only people can participate in government, civics, and economy. Only people have rights. When a collection of people organize themselves, this does not give them special rights over other groups of people, no matter how this group is organized. As being a corporation is only a collection of people, the corporation should act as such.

One method to change a corporation into a collective entity of individuals is ensuring every person within the collective is a shareholder, or owner of the corporation. The owner and employees share the same minimum wage per hour of work. This wage would be determined by the various levels of government, even down to the village level. The differences in compensation would be in the number of shares each person is entitled to. The number of shares would be determined by the corporation. To ensure the promotion of innovation and excellence, but also economic justice, varying levels of compensation are required. Using a progressive income tax system, any government can ensure income inequality does not reach unacceptable levels.

Another method to change a corporation is to make the corporation less "communistic" in its organization. For example, I find it quite ironic in the United States most corporations incorporate many aspects of communism, while promoting free market capitalism as its outward ideology. First, let's look into the perceived advantages of communism and whether or not corporations are supportive. Then we'll look into the perceived disadvantages of communism.

Advantages:
1. Efficient distribution of resources – Corporate shared goal
2. Equality – Depends on culture but for the most part, corporate shared goal
3. No competition – Corporate shared goal
4. Establishment of stronger communities – Not a shared corporate goal

5. Every citizen has a job – Not a shared corporate goal
6. Internally stable system – Shared corporate goal
Disadvantages:
1. Workers treated like machines – Usually a shared corporate goal
2. No individual freedom – Usually a shared corporate goal
3. Relying on fear – A subtly nuanced shared goal
4. Central planning of all means of production – Shared corporate goal
5. No constitution – Shared corporate goal
6. Religion marginalized or disallowed – Usually a shared corporate goal

Also it should be noted the most successive communist governments allow elections, although most do not allow elections. Corporations do not allow elections for management and are instead determined by a structured review process from echelons higher.

This type of study could be done comparing a corporate model to that of any form of government or economic system. As you can see, there are many characteristics common between a communist government and economy and the way corporations are currently organized. I would say much of the inefficiencies and issues related to an economy dominated by corporations is due to their structure. A free market cannot exist if the institutions and individuals comprising the free market are not themselves free.

Personally, I feel a corporation should be organized much like its government. Let me share why. A corporation administers justice. The powers of justice are limited but their effects can be more important than the powers administered by legislators, presidents, and judges. A corporation has direct control over pay, compensation, promotions, and the terms of your employment. These are forms of reward and punishment, the two pillars of any justice system implemented by a government. Governments regulate how a corporation may utilize these powers strictly or loosely, depending on the will of the people. Since a corporation, a collection of individuals, must administer justice with rewards and punishment, a corporation should also be recognized as a form of government. In fact, any collection of individuals which exercise reward AND punishment needs to be considered as government entities. It should be noted the very first corporation in the USA was financed by the English government under King James. This corporation was called the Virginia Company and was authorized to settle lands from modern day Massachusetts to Virginia and establish a government loyal to England. Even the religious pilgrims willingly helped the Virginia Company in these goals with a deal made to King James. King James allowed the Pilgrims freedom of religion and in repayment they pay taxes on all profits. We can witness components of this dynamic between American Protestantism, business, and government even today in every aspect of American culture.

Now, would it be acceptable to have a federal republic with smaller governments which are communist, fascist, or authoritarian? I anticipate any person answering this question would say no, this makes no sense. Others would of course avoid the answer and say the question has no merits. However, to me, this is part of the evolution of our intellect and a natural evolution of how we organize. If a corporation were organized like the government you allow to represent you, it would help empower your rights as an individual. Can a corporation be managed like a republic or democracy? I believe so. Trade unions try to provide some level of direct individual representation, but they also have very limited powers and effects.

Here is the summary of a proposed evolution of the corporation. A corporation is a governmental, for-profit entity where each person within the corporation shares in the profit to a minimum, yet varying degree.

This is just one idea. You may have other ideas. You may dislike this idea. This is okay. I invite you to partake in the evolution of our economic institutions at every level. Perhaps we can be more successful than gonorrhea in developing immunities to that which ails us within.

Chapter 18
A REVIEW OF CONSEQUENCES AND GOLDEN RULES

This chapter will review the seven consequences from Chapter 1 and the seven golden rules from Chapter 2 to consolidate the ideas presented in this book. Could the seven consequences be reduced or eliminated? Could the seven golden rules be improved or implemented? I will start with the consequences.

Consequence 1: The value of money must go up 2% forever. Implementing the Ency would allow for monetary growth, but not require monetary growth for economic success. With the Ency being energy based and part of a greater system which ensures each individual and family a means of producing or transforming energy, growth is not necessary for a good quality of life for all people. However, the foundations would be established where monetary growth could naturally occur without any manipulation from central banks. The key is the value of money itself would never fluctuate, but as more energy is produced and transformed, the more Ency will be produced. The result would be an equilibrium in the value of money, but a system of economic growth.

Consequence 2: The creation of money is an interlinked dynamic between banks, the government, and each manipulating the demand for the money. This link has not been completely broken through Ency implementation. There must be checks and balances in the entire system, much like some republics are set up. However, the proposal to eliminate the link by private banks playing a role in a governmental central bank is vital. Any money, especially a single world currency, needs to be as incorruptible as possible. This requires the elimination of a single private industry as the focal point of governmental policy. A government is made of people representing people and should represent the values and needs of the people. The proposals to create an institution involving people of many types of backgrounds would help identify the full needs of the entire spectrum of a people, not just a select few as is currently the case. The ability to manipulate demand for money would be eliminated by any central institution, allowing the true value of all goods and services to be realized in every nation.

Consequence 3: An entire economic system has been created to cater to exciting these passions and imaginations, which we have seen is extremely unstable. I honestly do not believe it is possible to eliminate the passions and imaginations of a population. Our inherent selves requires passion and imagination to live a full life and I never would want this eliminated. The implementation of the Ency would allow us to better measure the effects of our passions and imaginations from an economic view. The Ency will operate in a nearly closed system, as the entire world population would be using this currency. With Ency creation only happening when new energy is produced or transformed into a greater form, our decision making processes will be altered slightly. Sometimes the value of everything cannot possibly increase, meaning there could be situations where a reciprocal effect takes place. A reciprocal effect is when the value of one side increases while the value of another must decrease to the same degree. In an integrated economy, this could play out over a variety of goods and services. The only things where the value cannot decrease is any good which has a set energy output, like the example with the rice production. This baseline of value will ensure as our passions, imaginations, and desires change over time, we will still value agriculture and other forms of energy capture and production as much as we always have. This baseline can eliminate poverty without even requiring any type of welfare programs.

Consequence 4: No one knows the entire amount of debts they have. This book has not addressed an accounting system, or how debts would be managed. The main reflections on this subject included how historically, money was originally meant to be a mode of transaction instead of a storage of value. However, because money is a mode of transaction, it must have value. This requires money to be able to be a storage of value, although I believe there should be an incentive for people to invest money they have back into the economy instead of storing it. This is one of the main points of Keynesian economics I believe is vital. Should this investment also include the ability to make loans, or should all investment include sharing in the profit and loss of the investment. The main feature of implementing the Ency is accounting will be much simpler as compared to the current system. Instead of trying to maintain accounting records which must consider the constantly changing value of currencies, accounting can make a one-time entry into their books to express the value of the transaction. This can make complex business deals easier to navigate. Can debt itself be traded? Only if proper accounting is done. Maybe part of Ency implementation should include accounting reform.

Consequence 5: Most governments today, to include the most local governments of school districts, townships, counties, provinces, villages, cities, and so forth have unsustainable debts. This consequence actually troubles me more than most. If all the debts incurred by governments were added up, I feel it would almost be more than the actual value of all goods and services. Unfortunately there are no real numbers demonstrating either value. Creating the Ency by itself would not eliminate this problem, but this book did discuss a simplified taxation system focusing solely on individual income tax and a property tax. Each would be progressive and taxed by only the most local government. Higher echelons of government can only tax the lower echelon government's income and property in a progressive way. This simplification would make it easier for governments to budget their tax revenue. By having a system which itself can reduce and eliminate poverty, the burden for governments would be much less. They can focus on investments in infrastructure and education, which has direct benefit to an Ency economy. With a single world currency being used, governments throughout the world would be better integrated and in less competition with each other. This enhanced cooperation could help decrease the incentive to produce weapons. The use of weapons is destructive and reduces economic outputs. Reducing weapons expenditures would eliminate a great financial burden for governments. My hope would be for a government to have a balanced budget on average, with occasional surpluses in upward business cycles and occasional deficits in downward business cycles.

Consequence 6: Actions in society which are vital to the sustainability and progress of all mankind are steeped in neglect and poverty. Agriculture, education, and other vital activities often involve people who are poor. This is unacceptable. As discussed with some of the earlier consequences, these activities are part of energy production and transformation. As such, they will be valued more realistically closer to their real value. The Ency system itself ensure actions in society which are vital to the sustainability and progress of all mankind will not be neglected nor mired in poverty.

Consequence 7: Inequality, especially economic inequality, continues to increase. The Ency system would reduce income inequality. The pathway to this is fourfold. The first starts with the valuing of agricultural activities as energy production. The second is the simple and progressive taxation of income and property as determined by each government. The third is ensuring a minimum means of production and transformational capability to each person. The final one is allowing freedom of movement for people, not only the goods produced. These four things in tandem will reduce income inequality. There is still incentive to become wealthy, but their activities will also help bring up others in their community to a lesser degree. The incentive to earn more than others should never be eliminated as it is a way to reward quality and volume of work. Not each person is able to do equal quality and volume of work, and some prefer to devote less energy to their work. Given all these variabilities in human ability and desire, there should never be a system of purely equal pay for all. The best goal is to ensure one's wealth does not come from one's poverty. The Ency is the only economic system designed to do this within a free market economy.

Golden Rule 1: Acceptance on using money. The Ency system will continue to focus on this universal acceptance on using money. There is no need to make strict what even the greatest religious and ethical minds had allowed.

Golden Rule 2: Acceptance on working. The Ency system will encourage working for those able to do so by valuing each person's work for its true worth. This true worth ensures the incentive for work isn't merely survival, but to have a meaningful minimum quality of life.

Golden Rule 3: Encouragement to give charity. The Ency itself will not encourage any further charity than a person is already willing to provide through their own generosity. What the Ency will do is ensure there is a decreased need for charity by valuing human activity in a just manner. This isn't forced charity and people can still definitely give excess income, time, goods, and services as they deem appropriate. Also, the increased focus on community level government can increase a community's capacities by more closely integrating non-profits, business, and government to meet the needs of individuals and families within the community.

Golden Rule 4: Prohibitions on Usury. Usury has not been directly addressed, as debt is still able to be exist. There are certain features which should naturally limit usury. The first would be the access to a minimum means of energy production and transformation. Often times usury has been used to take advantage of situations where there was a need for immediate money but without an actual means to guarantee payment of this money, such as with payday loans. This means to production and transformation should reduce situations where money is immediately needed and also provide lenders a stronger guarantee for repayment. Also, with only a set supply of money in the market at any given time, and a guaranteed baseline for the valuation of the most basic goods such as food, the market may not be able to support widespread use of high interest rates. A more healthy financial market will exist since the valuations of all goods and services will be better known and people can better rely on the information they have. I would definitely still consider any additional direct regulation establishing acceptable interest rates if the Ency system itself still allows interest rates higher than is socially acceptable.

Golden Rule 5: Moderation. Moderation is the ultimate goal of the Ency system. The fourfold system described in consequence 7 earlier in this chapter should naturally lead to moderation. People will be encouraged to work together and live together. People won't be segregated based upon social status or other identifiable feature unless they choose to do so. Unforced integration at local levels and even at national levels will cause a greater realization into how interconnected we all are, while still promoting the importance of individual family units. A simple tax system will also ensure an inability of great excess at the cost of poverty. Finally, the Ency system is based upon an integrated approach to both the principles of science and faith, two of the best methods people worldwide accept in the regulation of human affairs and activity. By integrating both as a singular unit will ensure neither religion nor science is excessive nor neglected. Science without ethics leads to atomic bombs and sterilization programs, while religion without science creates holy crusades and the degradation of minority rights. Together though, moderation is the system.

Golden Rule #6: Detachment from material/physical things. The Ency system does not eliminate attachment to the material. The Ency can improve detachment though by ensuring each life and the activities each life endeavor towards has real value. The Ency places value on energy, which is a non-material thing empowering all which is material. This nuanced change may cause us to have a stronger attachment to the unseen forces whereupon all creation exists. It is a paradigm which will take time to shift, but I believe it would be inevitable.

Golden Rule #7: Debt is a promise. The Ency system does not do anything to ensure debt contracts and obligations are treated like a promise. Still, having a system in place which can ensure some type of guarantee to a means of production and minimum income can help offset the risks associated with lending. By providing a system which will ensure local level governments have greater influence than they do now, the interconnectedness could help restore the benefits of knowing your neighbors. When money is borrowed today, there is often uncertainty as to one's ability or willingness to pay. Both can be better resolved if financers and borrowers know each other better. Promises may still be broken, but communities can better regulate the effects of this broken promise. Also, eliminating usury will decrease the cost of borrowing so that the promise to repay is more reasonable and realistic.

To close this chapter, there is a solid foundation with the Ency. The Ency solves many of the problems currently afflicting society. Does it solve them all? No. The next and final chapter will discuss the most important way to fill in the gaps.

Chapter 19
A CALL FOR ACTION

I appreciate you taking the time to make it through this book. Part of my purpose in writing this goes well beyond simply making the case to implement a single world currency. Part of my purpose was to get your imagination going and to help transform your energy towards the elusive goal of unity. What good is an idea if there is no result?

The best possible result I could hope for is you want to be more involved in civic engagement with a hope of making your community, state, nation, and world a better place. I understand, though, that there could be any number of reactions you may have. You may disagree with my entire premise but find some nuggets of value. You may agree with my premise but disagree on some of the finer details. This is ok and is perfectly acceptable. No matter what, I ask that you be involved.

The goal for Unueco Partio is to create a new paradigm in the world body. This paradigm requires diversity, even diversity of thought, diversity of action, but all towards a unified goal. Think about your goals, imagine the goals of others, and assess them in regards to the current mode of doing things. Do the current economic and political systems help or hinder you in your true goals? Do they help or hinder you in your values? Do they help or hinder people you care about? If you find it difficult to answer "Yes" to these questions, be involved with Unueco Partio. Participate on the Facebook page, the forums, share your own ideas. Be constructive in your criticism and help refine the framework. Help create the bricks, doors, and windows that will fill in this framework. Unueco Partio needs you.

If you believe there is even one idea in this book worth considering, invite a friend to purchase the book and read it. Discuss these ideas with them. Ask how some of these ideas make one feel. I do not want to be the sole voice of Unueco Partio. I only want to be the founder and a representative.

If you choose to be a part of Unueco Partio, you probably will not earn more wealth than you do, if you earn any at all. There might be resistance by those who accept a system where profit is acceptable at the cost and potential misery of others. This will be a pathway which requires time, patience, and practice. Unueco Partio must operate more like a meditation working within the world. It isn't merely a revolution, it is a new way of living.

Unueco Partio will not censor you. All I ask is you express certain values to be a part of Unueco Partio. Be kind to others. Seek for others what you seek for yourself. This is all.

The second book for Unueco Partio will start focusing on government itself. What mode of government should Unueco Partio support? What would its constitution look like? What rights should people have and what powers should government have? I'll be evaluating these questions using the United Nations Declaration of Human Rights as the basis. As a preview, I will say I'm not 100% in agreement with this declaration. Thank you again for reading this. May the best be upon you.

ABOUT THE AUTHOR

Joshua W. Adams was born outside the small town of Palmyra, Illinois in the Midwestern United States. He first started working on a farm at the age of 14. Since then, he has been a sales manager, data analyst, warehouse manager, and a consultant for the lottery industry. His most important work was as an intelligence analyst while serving in the US Army for 8 years. Joshua never graduated from any university. He has always excelled at academic work but felt the institutions were too stifling and expensive. Instead Joshua has sought knowledge wherever he has been able to find it. Outside of professional life, Joshua enjoys playing basketball, video games, reading, and causing a little bit of trouble for those close to him. His combination of varied experiences and passionate belief in unity have led him to the path of becoming an author, a path he hopes to continue during his lifetime.

www.ingramcontent.com/pod-product-compliance
Lightning Source LLC
Chambersburg PA
CBHW050503290526
45786CB00006B/2410